VETERANS' STORII
ONE AMERICAN TC
SCITUATE, MASSACHUSETTS

M000031783

a TIME For WAR

Ronald Wheatley

HELLGATE PRESS   ASHLAND, OREGON

A TIME FOR WAR
©2015 Ronald Wheatley

Published by Hellgate Press
(An imprint of L&R Publishing, LLC)

All rights reserved. No part of this publication may be reproduced or
used in any form or by any means, graphic, electronic or mechanical,
including photocopying, recording, taping, or information and
retrieval systems without written permission of the publisher.

Hellgate Press
PO Box 3531
Ashland, OR 97520
email: sales@hellgatepress.com

Cover Design: Liz Wheatley
Interior Design: L. Redding

*Unless otherwise noted, all photos are from private collections provided
to the author by the interviewees and reproduced with permission.*

Printed and bound in the United States of America
First Edition 10 9 8 7 6 5 4 3 2 1

This book is dedicated to the memory of

Army Sergeant Michael J. Kelley and
Marine Recruit Coby Cutler.

And to all the veterans mentioned in this book and
elsewhere who have so nobly served their country.

Other Works by Ronald Wheatley

Books

A Song of Africa: The Roots of Boko Haram
(Named "Best Historical Novel" published
in 2011 by Books & Authors)

Plays/Docudramas

"The Trial of Phillis Wheatley"
(Winner of the 2015 eLit Award for Drama)

Essays

"Elusive Dreams"
(http://www.peacecorpswriters.org/pages/2004/0407/407warpeace.html)

CONTENTS

SECTION FOUR: THE KOREAN WAR

SECTION FIVE: THE COLD WAR

SECTION SIX: THE VIETNAM WAR

SECTION SEVEN: FIRST GULF WAR, IRAQ AND AFGHANISTAN

FIRST GULF WAR

IRAQ

AFGHANISTAN

SECTION EIGHT: 9/11

ABOUT THE AUTHOR............*353*

A TIME FOR WAR

Acknowledgments

MANY PEOPLE ARE INVOLVED IN THE CREATION OF A book. Their help is invaluable to an author in many ways including a push now and then during the long and slow journey from a blank piece of paper to a book. I would like to extend a word of thanks to those who helped me along the way in creating this book.

First I would like to thank the Community Newspaper Group, and the editors of the *Scituate Mariner* and *Cohasset Mariner* who published the articles I submitted under a column entitled "Calling All Veterans." To name a few who served as editors and were involved with fostering the column over the years: Bill Fonda, Kristi Funderburk, Nancy White, and Mary Ford of the *Cohasset Mariner*.

A special thanks to Pamela McCallum of Scituate who compiled the articles and offered encouragement as she brought them all together in the first PDF manuscript.

To my daughter, Elizabeth, who designed and created the cover.

To my editor and publisher, Harley Patrick, who agreed to publish the book.

To Brian Noble and Nobles Camera for their work with the reproductions of the many photos of veterans.

To Owen O'Malley, retired teacher from the Boston Latin School and attorney, who proofread the manuscript.

To the Chanticleer's Men's Club that meets in Hull and encourages its members to "stand up and tell your story."

To the many veterans—from privates and ordinary seamen to a four star general—who generously granted me the time to sit with them for an interview and without whose cooperation the book could never have been written.

To Lt. General Peter Kind, who heads the First Signal Brigade Association, and to New York playwright Kuros Charney, who both graciously provided the blurbs that appear on the back cover.

Thanks to the Scituate Knights of Columbus Council #3716 for the photo of Stuart Walker.

To my long-suffering wife, Ethel, who served as the first reader of the early versions of the articles before submission to the newspaper.

And I must mention my uncle, Ronald Joseph Herron, S.J., who elucidated me as my English teacher, trying to instill in me a respect for the simple declarative sentence and who as part of that process handed me a copy of *Judah Ben Hur: A Tale of the Christ* when I was thirteen and said, "Read this."

Introduction

THIS BOOK IS A COMPILATION OF INTERVIEWS that I have written over the past twenty years or so with veterans in the Town of Scituate, Massachusetts, and in some cases the contiguous town of Cohasset, Massachusetts. Being an attorney who practices in the area of estates, wills and trusts, I have a number of clients who were and are veterans. All of them have stories about their service days and they honored me by sharing their stories with me.

Having served in Vietnam as a communications specialist with the First Signal Brigade from June 1967 to June 1968, I was perhaps more interested than non-veteran attorneys might have been in these stories. But my interest in veterans has deeper roots still. On both my mother's and my father's side, family members have served in almost every war from the American Revolution to Iraq.

That tradition began with my great (six generations) grandfather, Leonard Wheatley of Virginia, who was serving with the Virginia militia, when the Continental Army was created in 1775. He ended by serving with General Washington's army as a private soldier on the continental line near Yorktown where he completed his service not long after General Cornwallis's surrender at Yorktown.

What I tried to do in all of these interviews was to ask the veterans about their civilian lives before the military, what motivated them to join, their training once in, and conclude with a little on their lives after their service.

After I had written the first article, I thought that these stories of local veterans might have a broader audience so I called the editor of the local newspaper, Bill Ketter, who at the time was the editor of the *Scituate Mariner*, part of a chain of newspapers serving a number of towns on the south shore of Boston. Mr. Ketter graciously agreed and thus began my column entitled "Calling All Veterans," which has run intermittently over the years up to today. I did not request or receive any remuneration for writing these articles, as this for me was a "labor of love."

These veterans' stories span the Civil War, World War II, Korea, Vietnam, Iraq and Afghanistan. In two instances, there are stories not based on interviews because there were no living veterans to be interviewed. In those cases I resorted to secondary sources, such as letters and historical records.

A number of the veterans from World War II that I interviewed have since passed, and this passage continues at an accelerated rate with the Korean War veterans as time takes its toll. I had no set purpose other than to interview veterans when I began this project. As I look back, though, I hope that these stories will provide some insight not only into the veteran's service but also the times when the veteran chose to serve. In any event one thing can be said of this effort, if nothing else, we saved their stories from the grave.

Ecclesiastes 3:1-8
A Time for Everything

[3] There is a time for everything,
and a season for every activity under the heavens:

[2] a time to be born and a time to die,
a time to plant and a time to uproot,

[3] a time to kill and a time to heal,
a time to tear down and a time to build,

[4] a time to weep and a time to laugh,
a time to mourn and a time to dance,

[5] a time to scatter stones and a time to gather them,
a time to embrace and a time to refrain from embracing,

[6] a time to search and a time to give up,
a time to keep and a time to throw away,

[7] a time to tear and a time to mend,
a time to be silent and a time to speak,

[8] a time to love and a time to hate,
a time for war and a time for peace.

New International Version (NIV) Holy Bible, New International Version®, NIV®
Copyright ©1973, 1978, 1984, 2011 by Biblica, Inc.®
Used by permission. All rights reserved worldwide.

A TIME FOR WAR

SECTION ONE

THE REVOLUTIONARY WAR

A TIME FOR WAR

Unpopular Wars

Leonard Wheatley

"The reflection upon my situation and that of this army produces many an uneasy hour. When all around me are wrapped in sleep, few people know the predicament we are in. General George Washington, January 14, 1776."

So begins the audio version of the book *1776* by David McCullough.

With February 22 being George Washington's birthday, it is appropriate to take a moment to reflect on some of our earliest veterans.

In retrospect it is difficult for some to realize that the Revolutionary War was not a popular one—with approximately one third of the population supporting the break with England, by force if necessary, one third remaining staunchly loyal to England and King George III, and one third retaining a neutral position. And as the war dragged on with defeat after defeat, retreat after retreat, privation after privation, it became even less popular. Americans don't like prolonged conflicts.

As Charles Dickens wrote: "It was the best of times, it was the worst of times, it was the age of wisdom, it was

Leonard Wheatley's grave stone in Breckenridge, Kentucky, near his ancestral home.

the age of foolishness…it was the spring of hope, it was the winter of despair…in short, the period was so far like the present…."

I had an ancestor who had served in the army during that war. His name was Leonard Wheatley and he was my great, great, great grandfather. According to his records, which I have, he had to wait a long, long time to receive any veteran's benefits.

On November 17, 1845, at the age of eighty, many years after he had originally applied and been turned down for a pension because he had lost his discharge papers, he appeared before the Court of Breckinridge County

(Kentucky) and made a solemn declaration in order to obtain the benefit of the Pension Act Congress passed June 7, 1832.

His statement reflects the fact that he entered the services in the Militia of Virginia in the month of May 1780. He entered as a substitute for his brother John Wheatley under a Captain Evans and served a tour of three months. He lived in Prince William County, Virginia when he entered the service.

According to his records he was first marched to a little town called Dumphries on Quantico Creek and remained there about a month and then marched to Falmouth (Virginia), there to Hunters Works and guarded there three or four weeks. He was then marched to Dumphries and there dismissed.

In July 1781 he again entered the service as a substitute for one Charles Coppage. He was then ordered to march up to Colchester where they met General George Washington with the army coming down to Yorktown, and then he was ordered back to Yorktown. He was dismissed about the time General Cornwallis surrendered.

But duty called again when one Alexander MacDonald asked Wheatley to substitute for his sick brother. He then marched to Falmouth and met the British prisoners and marched them up to a barracks near Falmouth where he remained as a guard for some time.

The records name all of his commanders during these periods for authentication purposes. They point out that he knew General Morgan, General Knox, and saw General George Washington, but was not long with many of the regular officers.

But justice was finally done for Wheatley when that Court of Breckinridge County ruled: "[We] hereby declare…that after investigation of the matter, and after putting the interrogation prescribed by the War Department, that the above named applicant was a revolutionary soldier and served as he states…as a private soldier in the army of the United States in the war of the Revolution, and that he is now a Pensioner of the United States…at the rate of twenty dollars per annum." The court also awarded him the pension back pay from the time he first applied.

The Civil War was unpopular, and so were Korea and Vietnam. I know a little about unpopular wars having served in Vietnam from 1967-1968. But would America exist today if she had not participated in unpopular wars?

Now we are engaged in another unpopular war, and this fate of my family follows, as our son, Lance Corporal John Wheatley, who is a graduate of Norwich University in Vermont and a manager at AVID Corporation in Tewksbury, has been activated and will leave for Fallujah, Iraq, next month with approximately 1,000 men and women of the 1st Battalion, of the 25th Marines Regiment, New England's only Marine Reserve Unit. We hope and pray for their safe return.

I look forward to the day my son will march with me in Scituate's Memorial Day Parade as a member of Scituate VFW Post and Scituate's to-be-reconstituted American Legion Post # 144.

SECTION TWO

THE CIVIL WAR

A TIME FOR WAR

Letters from the Siege of Petersburg

William Reuben and James Andrews

"SCITUATE SENT TWO HUNDRED AND SIXTY-FOUR MEN into the Union army and navy during the Civil War. The biggest recruitment drive was in the late summer of 1862. Most of the Army recruits went to the 35th Massachusetts Regiment. About thirty men did not return mostly because of disease," writes local historian and member of the Satuit Camp Number 3188 of the Sons of Union Veterans, David E. Corbin. Among those Scituate recruits were James, William and Reuben Andrews. According to Corbin, "James died of disease at Falmouth VA on February 4, 1863."

As in every war the ordinary enlisted rank has no idea of the grand schemes that the "Gods and Generals" draw up in the step-by-step campaign to achieve their ultimate goal. The ordinary soldier just follows orders, marching from place to place, digging defensive positions, and engaging the enemy when ordered. Such was the case of the surviving Andrews brothers, William and Reuben, who in June of 1864 found themselves far from home.

William Andrews is the top image, James is below. According to the Andrews family, three brothers—William, James and Reuben—all enlisted in the 35th Mass. Regiment and served in the same infantry comapany.

Little did the brothers, nor for that matter their general officers, know that they were part of what would become a 292 day duel of artillery, mortars and rifle fire that evolved into trench warfare presaging that of WWI—the Siege of Petersburg. From June 9, 1864 to March 25, 1865, Union forces in a series of battles struggled to take Petersburg, a strategic location and rail center in the heart of the Confederacy. Union forces slowly cut off Petersburg from the world and brought the fall of the Confederacy.

For William, like most soldiers, family and home were the highest priorities. With brother James already dead, he takes on a special responsibility for brother Reuben serving at his side, and the family's finances in Scituate. The dateline of each letter reflects movement— the shift of Camps in attacking the City:

Camp near Big Black, July 6, 1864: Dear Parents: Well at last of a surety Vicksburg has fallen. We heard the great news on Friday and the 4th it was confirmed. We also received on the 4th a stunning big mail, the first for five weeks. As you may suppose I came in for a goodly share....I sent fifteen dollars (home) and twelve from Reuben...We are now awaiting orders and are about two miles from the Big Black River where a fight is expected if Johnston does not "skedaddle" which I rather think he will as I think we out-number. He is said to be in force about 10 miles across the river. I do not think we shall be engaged...We have done nothing since we arrived with the exception of four days' work digging rifle pits of which we have two lines to fall back if we are obliged to fall back... Marching is very hard work here. We started about six o'clock on the fourth and reached the place where we are now about six last night—a distance of only about seven miles. This was partly owing to the great heat and dust as partly to bad roads over which our artillery passed with great difficulty and we were obliged to halt to allow them to keep up with us. The climate has not taken hold of me yet...No more at present from your son, William...All is well as usual.

The second letter dated about a month later is from a camp at "the gates of the City":

Petersburg August 14th '64: Dear Father: At last we have been paid and on Friday afternoon I sent you forty dollars, together with thirty from Reuben. I except I have not much to write for everything continues about in the usual course. We have the regular picket firing and an occasional artillery duel....The Corps is under orders to move at a moment's notice and it is expected by many that we shall move up on the right. The regiment started a new fort last night and the rebs put in a shell within 10 feet of our company. It was within an arm's length of where Phinney (of Cohasset) was, but fortunately he escaped uninjured. The explosion covered our whole company with dirt. A second round struck in nearly the same place but luckily did not explode. My opinions about reenlisting remain about the same as I have stated before...Lt. Farrington is in command of the regiment as present, Capt. Ingals having gone to hospital on account of the breaking out of his wound received at Antietam. No more at present, from your son, W.B.D. Andrews."

In his last letter William writes":

Nicholasville, Aug. 30th: I am well and so also is Brother Reuben and at present enjoying ourselves hugely...You speak of not being able to save any of our wages...do not want for anything for the sake of saving for me for if I get through this safe I think I can do something to keep the thing (farm) going...

Tell mother that (I and Reuben) are both alive and showing to be pretty good soldiers...Wishing you good luck with your gardening and also (that) your large brood may be blessed with good health...From your affectionate son, William.

A month later, William's corps was ordered to cut the last rail line into Petersburg, Virginia. William Andrews was killed at the battle of Poplar Springs Church. The attempt to cut the rail line was unsuccessful. Rueben's fate is the subject of more research.

A TIME FOR WAR

SECTION THREE

WORLD WAR TWO

A TIME FOR WAR

A Legacy of Service

Frannie Litchfield

I am closing my 52 years of military service. When I joined the Army, even before the turn of the century, it was the fulfillment of all of my boyish hopes and dreams. The world has turned over many times since I took the oath at West Point, and the hopes and dreams have all since vanished, but I still remember the refrain of one of the most popular barracks ballads of that day which proclaimed most proudly that old soldiers never die; they just fade away. And like the old soldier of that ballad, I now close my military career and just fade away, an old soldier who tried to do his duty as God gave him the light to see that duty, Goodbye

—General Douglas MacArthur

A S A BOY SCOUT I WAS PRIVILEGED TO HEAR General MacArthur make that speech, not the one before the joint session of Congress, but rather when he was on a speaking tour in Seattle.

Old soldiers become old Veterans, young soldiers become young Veterans, but all too soon they also become old Veterans, and they too eventually fade away.

An older gentlemen friend tells me that he remembered when he was a young boy seeing Civil War

Frannie Litchfield

veterans riding in a horse drawn wagon down Front Street one Memorial Day many, many years ago. Think of all the tales those veterans could have told about their service, Bull Run, Antietam, Gettysburg, but there was no one there to memorialize those memories. They just faded away.

Today our old soldiers, our old veterans are fading away. The number of World War II veterans marching in the Memorial Day parade dwindles each year. We need to preserve their memories.

One such "old soldier" is Frannie Litchfield of Scituate.

"I served from June of 1942 to November of 1945," Litchfield said speaking of his service as an aircraft mechanic/electrician with the then U.S. Army Air Corp stationed at an airfield in Cha Bua in Northern India at the foot of the Himalayan Mountains.

"The runway there was the only paved spot in the whole area. We serviced C-87s, which were four engine B-24 bombers converted to carry cargo. Their mission was to fly over the 'Hump' at an altitude of thirty-two thousand feet to get over the Himalayan Mountains. They carried supplies, munitions, and gasoline from India to China."

According to Litchfield his outfit carried so much material in one month that it received a Presidential Unit Citation in December of 1944.

"There were two seasons, the monsoons and the dry season, but it was always hot. Inside the aircraft the temperature averaged 108 degrees. During the monsoons you wished it was the dry season and during the dry season you wished it was the monsoon season."

Litchfield wanted to fly but an ear infection kept him on the ground.

"We lost many aircraft," Litchfield said, "mostly on takeoff and landing. At one time, out of a contingent of thirty-two aircraft we were down to three on the ground and three still flying; all the rest had crashed. Some crews survived by being able to parachute out. One crew who bailed out took forty-two days to make it back to the base. We also had some fighter planes there, Spitfires, I think, and one day one pilot crashed all three."

The men lived in mud huts with thatched roofs—ten men to a hut.

"One day one of the aircraft belly landed. All the crew got out except the pilot whose foot was caught in the wreckage of the cockpit. We were always afraid of fire, so I grabbed a fire ax and began chopping away at the airframe so that I could get into the plane to free the pilot's foot. I guess it might have been the first version of the 'jaws of life.' While I was chopping away at the fuselage, a major came by and reprimanded me. I don't want to say what I told him, but needless to say I continued chopping to create a space large enough for me to crawl through, and free the pilot's leg before the plane caught fire."

Litchfield represents a long line of military men with a grandfather who served in the Civil War, a father who was in the First World War; sons who served during the Vietnam era, a submariner grandson, and another relative who just returned from Iraq.

"I would not trade my service for a million dollars," Litchfield said, "but I can't say I would want to go through it again."

A Man for All Seasons

Clyde Gurney

EARLY IN THE MORNING THREE TIMES A WEEK he brings freshly cut long stem red Amaryllis for display to the French Memories in Cohasset. There he commandeers his favorite table for his morning coffee and pastry. Long time Scituate resident Clyde Gurney also delivers his flowers to Oro's Restaurant, and the South Shore Hospital cardiac center. He is well known as a gardener and bird lover. It takes patience and dedication to nurture a virtual green house of over a hundred bulbs and plants at various stages of development in your home during the long winter months. But there is another side of his life, of his patience, not chronicled. He longed to serve in the Navy during World War II; a goal denied him almost half a decade.

"My father was from England and my mother from Scotland and that is how I got the name Clyde—for the Perth of Clyde in Scotland."

Gurney attended Rockland high school where he was a straight A student because, as he puts it, "I had an excellent memory." Gurney graduated from high school in 1935.

Clyde Gurney

"I was lucky to get a job," Gurney said. "It was with the HH Arnold company in Rockland manufacturing weaponry. I was working on brass casings for shells. The owner of the company actually got involved in teaching me the necessary technical skills to do the job."

In 1939 while working for the company Gurney received a draft notice, and he tried to enlist in the Navy.

"The building where we worked in Rockland had all the windows painted black. We would work all night long. Because the company was fulfilling a War Department contract, they wanted to keep me deferred."

The months at the plant turned to years while many of Gurney's mates went off to serve in the war. "I was wondering how I would answer the question 'What did you do during the war?'"

"I finally pleaded with my boss to let me go. I told him all my buddies were in the service and I wanted to serve."

In 1944, his employer finally granted him leave to go and serve on active duty. He had waited nine years.

"I joined the Navy in 1944 and went to boot camp at Sampson in New York." After boot camp, Gurney was selected for a top-secret research project that the Navy was working on in conjunction with Harvard and Columbia.

"I was assigned to the USS *Babbitt*. It was a World War I destroyer. We were carrying out scientific research in sonar under battle conditions."

According to Gurney, at that time Harvard and Columbia had taken a lead in the study of underwater sound—sonar.

"We would sail from Port of Spain, Trinidad to Greenland, and there would be a submarine shooting dummy torpedoes underneath us so we could check the sonar readings under cold/warm water conditions."

The stark contrast of the ship's route still impresses him.

"So we would be down in Port of Spain listening to the workers singing 'Rum and Coca Cola / Working for the Yankee dollar,' and then we would go up to Greenland where we would be surrounded by huge icebergs that towered over our ship."

Gurney admits to bouts of seasickness.

"I did a lot of cooking on ship as well. When we were in port, I would do the cooking so that the cooks could be able to get off the ship."

After three years of service in the Navy, Gurney was honorably discharged in 1947. He returned to the same company where he been employed since 1935. He became highly skilled in the craft of precision cylindrical grinding.

"When I first went there we were working to a thousandth of an inch, and when I retired we were working at a millionth of an inch."

Part of Gurney's work took him to Switzerland where he would buy advanced machines for the company.

"I bought a 1790 home in Middleboro on sixteen acres for $12,000, and spent five years restoring it. It had four fireplaces. I married in the early '70s. My bride, Mimi Cohen, was from Casablanca. Her brother was a chef at some of the top French restaurants in Boston, and introduced me to that world. I built a barbecue. I put in a swimming pool." It was there that he hosted Sunday barbecues for the Boston restaurateurs and guests.

Gurney retired in 1970. "I worked in the same place for 65 years—from 1935 to 2000—with a three year stint in the Navy. When I first came to Scituate in 1972, I went to Widows Walk and over to Marshfield Country Club and put in birdhouses. I have always been into birding."

By April his oriental lilies will be ready, followed by the tulips. As the seasons change Gurney changes his flower deliveries.

A Red Cross Volunteer
in World War II

Estelle Adler

U NLIKE THE MANY WHO JOINED UP TO SERVE in World War II right out of high school, when long time Scituate resident Estelle Adler made the existential decision to serve, she had already had a successful career in communications in both the private and public sectors—a career that began in Boston right after college in 1938.

"In 1938, I became the traffic manager for radio station WORL in Boston. I transferred to WBZ," Adler said. "The WBZ station manager was named the Director of Radio, Press and Advertising for War Bonds in a newly created special branch of the Treasury Department." According to Adler, this new position took him to Washington D.C., and before long Adler followed.

"From October 1942 to January 1944, I worked for the War Savings Division of the United States Treasury Department in the Radio, Press and Advertising section."

Estelle Adler in World War II serving
as a Red Cross volunteer.

There could have been few places in the world as
adult as Washington, D.C., during World War II. Adler
was right in the middle of it.

"One of my responsibilities was to serve on a round
table comprised of some of the leading generals' wives.
I would coordinate coffees for them, including Mrs.
Eisenhower, Mrs. George Patton, and Mrs. Mark Clark."
Adler's job was to interact with people—especially with
those who could help raise War Bond money.

"We interacted with the 'Hollywood Canteen' and I
worked with celebrities including such stars as Paul

Henried, Loretta Young, and Groucho Marx," Adler said. But the out-reach extended beyond Hollywood to world famous artists such as Italian Conductor Arturo Toscanini, and to world statesmen, such as when British Prime Minister Winston Churchill came to the United States to address a joint session of congress.

"Young men—friends of mine from New England—kept showing up in Washington…[they were] writers from the Office of War Information, and I became even more concerned and interested in the war," Adler said. "So I approached the Marines. Anyway, no one would send me anywhere outside this country. Then I heard about the Red Cross, and sure enough early in 1944, I joined and I left Washington to go overseas."

Adler was part of a contingent of "125 Red Cross girls" who sailed unescorted and unaware of their destination out of New York on the Queen of the Cunard Lines—the *Mauritania*. "It was a fast ship, able to outmaneuver German U-boats. Off the shores of Ireland, the ship suddenly started wild gyrations, and I soon found out we were outrunning German submarines. At that moment I asked myself: What am I doing here?"

"We sailed to North Africa—Oran and Algiers. We met with soldiers at the canteens and worked with Army Special Services at dances and other events," Adler said.

"From Algiers I went to the island of Corsica, which was my first actual assignment. There I opened and closed three different clubs. We would take over a building and wash it down. Get coffee pots, magazines, a piano and it would become a focal point for the soldiers. In Corsica we were serving veterans who had served at Anzio. I was in Corsica when the Allies invaded southern France. I watched 'Wild' Bill Donovan's OSS troops working out at the beach at night prior to the invasion."

In the midst of the war, there was still glamour. "While I had to 'DDT' my way to my mosquito netted bed in my quarters, my Red Cross friend stayed at the palatial Napoleon Bonaparte Hotel. I used to go to lunch with her. We would see Randolph Churchill, who was reputed to be a spy, and Douglas Fairbanks Jr., who was with the Royal Navy. I was present with a contingency from a French hospital relocated from Paris the night Paris was liberated."

Following another assignment in Naples, "I was reassigned to Florence as the resident director of the Apollo Theatre, a 4,200 seat theatre and movie house," Adler said. "I would order films. I booked the best USO shows. Our most popular show was a baseball show with Stan Musial and 'Lippy' Leo Durocher, famed manager of the Brooklyn Dodgers. The service men loved the baseball show." During this period we created our own theater company and I starred in two shows, 'Margin for Error,' and 'Love Rides the Rails.'

"The war ended for me May 8th in Florence, Italy. In July 1945, I married a British officer, who served in the Indian Army. We came to Scituate in 1946."

Adler had five children, two boys and three girls, and has eight grandsons, three great grandsons, and one great granddaughter. She has been active in civic endeavors, including the "Scituate Dramateurs." She retired as Public Relations Director from Massasoit College. In 1989, Adler served as a Public Information Officer for the Federal

Estelle poses in her Red Cross uniform while holding a photo from her time in service during World War II.

Emergency Planning Administration (FEMA) out of Region One headquartered in Boston. Among the disasters she worked on-site were the San Francisco earthquake in 1989 and the Los Angeles earthquake in 1992.

Adler is the granddaughter of Thomas Murray who served with the Massachusetts 5th Infantry in the Civil War. Recently at a meeting of the Scituate Sons of Union Veterans, she donated her grandfather's military papers and other civil war memorabilia to Satuit Camp 3188.

A TIME FOR WAR

A Tradition of Service

John "Jack" Whitney

A CONTINENT AWAY, AND ALMOST TWO YEARS before that fateful shell "screamed and fell," there's a story to tell. It is the story of one of the members of the entire sophomore class at Bates College in Lewiston, Maine, who enlisted in the armed services about a year after the attack on Pearl Harbor. Early in his Army training, this then young man volunteered to become an Army Ranger. This is his story.

"We landed on the beach at Marseille at night, said John "Jack" Whitney of Scituate. "I was a tech sergeant in charge of a platoon of about thirty Army Rangers. I was in charge of "Easy Company" comprised of members of our group, the 63rd Infantry Division, and joined by some members of the 3rd Army Division. It was around the end of 1943 when we went in. The Vichy French who were in control of the City had scuttled boats in the harbor to hamper our landing, but we made it ashore. Our mission was to pursue the Germans who were leaving the area."

John "Jack" Whitney in the spring of 2008
at his home in Scituate, Massachusetts.

Whitney led "Easy Company" in pursuit of the
Germans north toward the German border. "There was
heavy fighting all the way," Whitney said. The Germans
had occupied Colmar and were waiting. "When we
reached Strasbourg, we thought we were going to cross
the Rhine, but no, we were sent south to near the German
border."

He recalls one village that they went through along the way which the Germans occupied. "We fought a three day house-to-house battle and we took many casualties." Whitney modestly admits his group was awarded a Presidential Unit citation for that battle. After that battle Tech Sergeant Whitney was awarded a battlefield commission as a second lieutenant.

As if things weren't bad enough, according to meteorological data, the winter of 1944 was one of the coldest on record in Europe. Whitney and his men fought on in some of the harshest conditions on their long march.

"I ordered the men to keep two dry pair of socks under their jackets so if their feet got wet they could change into dry socks to prevent frostbite and trench foot."

As orders changed, Whitney's objective became a section of the Siegfried Line where the Germans had used French slave labor to build cement abutments called "Tigers' Teeth"—Jersey barrier type obstacles—designed to stop tanks from entering Germany from France.

"As we approached our objective we had to march up toward a ridge line though an area of heavy forest. At the top of the ridge, the Germans had built pillboxes with overlapping fields of fire." As Whitney led his company up the snowy hill, 105 millimeter shells pounded the forest sending lethal shrapnel and sharp tree shards in every direction.

"I heard the 105 coming, and I had the time to roll myself into a ball." The shell slammed into a nearby tree and Whitney was hit by the shrapnel. Whitney's twenty-three month military career was over.

"I was evacuated to a field hospital and then onto another hospital in Birmingham, England. While I was there, we heard the war in Europe had ended."

His Division suffered about 3,000 casualties during the long and arduous march. As a result of his injuries, Whitney was put in a body cast, and eventually shipped home to an Army hospital where he spent about a year.

He "retired" from the Army as a first lieutenant. For his action in World War II, Whiney was awarded the Purple Heart and the Bronze Star, among other medals.

Whitney, who lives in Scituate, and his late wife, Jeanne, raised their family here, and he remains close to his daughters, Dianne and Sharon, and his son, John.

His family boasts a proud tradition of military service with his father, John, having served in World War I, and then contributing to World War II by working in the Quincy Shipyard. His son, John, followed in the family tradition serving with distinction in Vietnam as a member of an elite team of Long Range Recon soldiers. For his services, like his father, Whitney junior was highly decorated.

Following his World War II military service, Whitney retuned to college and received a master's degree in history and government. He had a long career in Weymouth with the Minnesota Mining Company.

A Triumph of Spirit

Mary Regan Quessenberry

"WORLD WAR II BROKE OUT IN DECEMBER 1941, and I was in uniform by July of 1942. I joined with the very first group of women to enter into the military. We were called the Women's Army Auxiliary Corps ("WAAC"). There was prejudice against women serving in the military," said Mary Regan Quessenberry, a longtime resident of Scituate. She is pictured with her group in the coffee table book published by *Life* magazine entitled "Our Finest Hour, The Triumphant Spirit of America's World War II Generation." The caption to the picture reads: "WAAC's soon to be WAC's practice close order drill across parade ground at Fort Des Moines."

Daughter of an MIT graduate engineer father, John W. Regan, and mother, Mary Veronica Sullivan, a graduate from Radcliffe, Quessenberry was raised in Boston. She praises her parents for instilling in her the desire to learn and helping her attain a fine education. By the time America entered the war Quessenberry had graduated from Radcliffe majoring in fine arts, traveled around the world as part of fellowship to study in China and Japan,

Mary Regan Quessenberry

and had earned a master's degree in Fine Art from Harvard. Both her older brother, John, and her younger brother, Robert, trained as physicians at Harvard and Tufts respectively, and served with distinction in World War II.

"In July of 1942, we were sent to Fort Des Moines," she said. "We were the 'Six Week Wonder Girls' and I was commissioned a third officer WAAC. Upon graduation I stayed on to train the 'new girls.'" Following that stint, "I volunteered to return to Boston to recruit for what had become the Women's Army Corps (WACs). I had learned that Winston Churchill was coming to receive an honorary degree at Harvard. I was standing on the steps of the Fogg Museum. I saw a couple of big black limousines pull up. Prime Minister Winston Churchill exited one car with his wife—later to become Lady Churchill—and their daughter, Mary. Lady Churchill saw me standing there in uniform, approached and she commented on being delighted to see women in uniform. I have a picture posing with Mary Churchill there.

"Not long after that, in 1943, I received orders to go overseas. I was so happy," Quessenberry said. "I was ordered to attend a photo interpreter school near High Wickham (headquarters of the British Bomber Command), up the Thames from London where I was trained to assess bomb damage from aerial photographs following bomb raids. While there, I was part of the United States Army 8th Air Force which then was commanded by Three Star General James 'Jimmy' Doolittle.

"After training, I was sent to the Royal Air Force (RAF) Base at Medmenham near London." The Central Interpretation Unit was located there and it was involved in almost every operation of the war, including almost every aspect of military intelligence. "We operated twenty-four hours a day, and had to assess the damage to German aircraft from the bombing raids. Our reports were of an urgent nature and had to be provided to the commands that would be flying the next day so they would know what to expect as to fighter opposition.

"Late one evening, I was called to report to Twickenham, the highest headquarters led by General Carl Spaatz who commanded the strategic bombing campaign against Germany. General Spaatz' command by then included the 8th, 9th and 15th Army Air Corps and he reported to General Eisenhower. I served there for two years. I was company commander of 550 WAC's who ran Spaatz Headquarters."

Quessenberry's service during that time is best summed up by the citation that accompanies her Bronze Star, which states in part: "For meritorious service in connection with military operations as commanding officer of an Air Force Women's Army Corp detachment...during the critical period of enemy flying bomb attacks in Southern England. Her leadership and devotion to duty facilitated to a great extent the rapid and efficient move of headquarters to France and establishment of full operations at the new location. Her commendable services reflect great credit upon herself and the Women's Army Corps."

At the cessation of hostilities, Quessenberry participated in the Victory in Europe (VE) Day parade in Paris. Following a brief Rest and Recuperation at home, she returned to Berlin for two more years to serve as head of Intelligence in a newly created Division under the command of General Lucius D. Clay, in a new kind of war to rescue and repatriate precious works of art. These art works were looted from German occupied countries such as Italy, France, and the Netherlands by the Nazis' special squad of art advisors established by Adolph Hitler—the Einsatztab Reichsleiter Rosenberg (ERR). Quessenberry's work included travel to salt mines, abandoned factories, and bombed cities, in Germany, Austria, Poland and other countries. The responsibilities of the command were also to identify monuments, and buildings that needed preservation.

Following that period, Quessenberry returned home

to lecture at the University of Florida where she met her husband to be, Tim, and they married in 1965. Widowed in 1978, Quessenberry resides at her ancestral home in Scituate.

"I always felt that the Bronze Star I was awarded should have gone to a nineteen-year-old soldier in a foxhole near Bastogne (during the Battle of the Bulge)," Quessenberry said.

A TIME FOR WAR

A Very Special Christmas

Stuart Walker

T HE CHRISTMAS SEASON HAS A SPECIAL MEANING for
Stuart Walker, long time Scituate resident, his wife,
and family. "We sailed for Hawaii on Christmas Eve,
1944," Walker said.

But this story really begins three years earlier when
the Japanese attacked Pearl Harbor on December 7,
1941. Then a recent high school graduate, Walker was
working in a defense plant and had a draft deferment. He
married his high school sweetheart, Ann, on December
12, 1941, five days after Pearl Harbor, and two weeks
before Christmas.

"My best friend enlisted in the Marines, and I wanted
to follow him. My bride wasn't happy about that, so I
volunteered for the Coast Guard—with her permission—
since at that time the wife had to sign off on such
enlistments," Walker said. "I was rejected because I was
six foot three, and the Coast Guard limit was six foot two,"
Walker says with a smile and a shrug. Throughout his
military career, he would encounter many such "Situation
Normal—All Fouled Up" occasions (aka known as

KOFC
CHARITY RAFFLE
$100.00 PER TICKET
ONLY 500 SOLD
DRAWING HERE
SATURDAY NIGHT
WINNER NEED NOT BE
PRESENT

WIN
$10,000
RAFFLE
BUY
TICKETS
HERE

Stuart Walker working at one of the booths at the annual carnival sponsored by the Scituate Knights of Columbus Council #3716. Walker was a long-time faithful volunteer at this annual charity event.

SNAFUs). Shortly thereafter, the Coast Guard changed its height requirements and Walker was accepted. "After boot camp at Manhattan Beach, I was assigned to teach 'seamanship,' which I knew nothing about." It was another one of those SNAFUs.

"Just then there was the first service-wide selection for officer training available to all Coast Guard enlisted personnel. I applied and was selected. I spent three months training at the Coast Guard Academy" [in New London, Connecticut]. "I graduated, receiving a commission as an ensign in November 1943," Walker said. "My first assignment was to a weather ship operating out of Boston."

Walker recounts that first patrol out of Boston: "The escort tug was delayed and the captain of the tug—an impatient ex-Merchant Mariner —shouted: 'l will take her out myself.' In the process of taking her out, the captain also took out part of the dock, and seriously damaged the ship's propellers. We proceeded to sail for four hours before the damaged propellers caused a bearing to wear out." Undaunted, the captain ordered the crew to repair the ship at sea. "We made another four hours before the other bearing went. Somehow we made it back to Boston for repairs, but after the repairs were completed, the ship was promptly decommissioned." It was another one of those mysterious military SNAFUs that Walker was encountering with frightening regularity.

"From the weather ship, I was assigned to the Coast Guard Amphibious Forces at Camp Bradford near Norfolk, Virginia for training as a gunnery officer on a Landing Ship Tank 'LST.' After completing my gunnery officer training, I was assigned to LST 880 as a communications officer," Walker said. LSTs were amphibious vessels that transported troops and supplies. They would nose up on the beach head where the huge clam shell bow doors would open, disgorging men and equipment; then back off as quickly as possible. "Nosing up and backing off was a complex process dependent on time and tides," Walker said.

"A few days out of Hawaii, a slot for a communications officer on the Command ship, LST 770, opened up, and I took it," Walker said, not knowing at the time of the consequences of his fateful decision. With approximately five and half months of sea duty, on Easter Sunday 1945, Walker was about to play a key role in a momentous event. "I was at my station high up in the conning tower of the lead ship 'conning' it toward, and onto, the beach," in what would become the largest amphibious battle in the Pacific in World War II—the Battle of Okinawa.

"We quickly unloaded the men and equipment under fire, and backed out to sea to sail to the Philippines, get another load, and return. We made half a dozen such round trips. During one landing as the man on the highest point of the ship, I saw a Kamikaze plane headed right for me, but at the last minute he changed course flying about ten feet over my head for a better target."

The LSTs' role in the Okinawa completed, "We were on our way to participate in the invasion of Japan when the atomic bomb was dropped on Hiroshima on August 6, 1945," Walker said.

After many delays, including "sailing through a typhoon as we were bound for Seattle, and being snow bound on trains in the Rockies and Appalachian mountains, I finally made it home on the anniversary of my sailing for Hawaii. I surprised my wife decorating the tree on Christmas Eve 1945. It was a wonderful reunion."

Following his service, Walker took advantage of the GI Bill, graduated as a mechanical engineer from Stoner's

Institute of Technology in Hudson, New Jersey. Eventually, his career in industrial sails brought him to Scituate in 1954. He and Ann are the parents of two sons and a daughter who live nearby, the grandparents of six, and great grandparents of one. Walker, a onetime Scituate School Board member, has been active coaching Scituate Little League, the Scituate Knights of Columbus, and the Scituate Adult Music Booster Association to support music in the schools. "I served my country in an ordinary way— as millions of others have," Walker says of his service. LST-770 was awarded one battle star for her service during World War II.

A TIME FOR WAR

"Coastie"

John Sieminski

"I BEAT THE DRAFT BY TWO DAYS. ON JULY 1ST, 1942, I had received a notice to report to the Army on the following Saturday. On Tuesday, I traveled to Pittsburg, Pennsylvania [which was near where he lived] to enlist in the Coast Guard. I told the recruiter of my draft notice, but he just told me to come back on Thursday, that there was a contingent of recruits shipping out that day for Boot Camp," said John Sieminski of Scituate.

Sieminski spent six weeks at boot camp at Curtis Bay, Maryland, near Baltimore, and then was chosen to go with a group to the Boston Coast Guard Receiving Station.

Once in Boston the men were told we were being assigned to Scituate.

"We all thought that meant we were being assigned to a ship, the 'U.S.S. *Scituate*,'" Sieminski said. But he, along with some others, ended up at the Coast Guard Station at First Cliff. It was at that station where Sieminski served a year doing beach patrol, walking with rifles from First Cliff to the North River and back—a two

John Sieminski on patrol as a Coast Guardsman on the beach in Scituate early in World War II. At the time, there were concerns of a possible invasion on the beaches of the East Coast.

hour patrol—and from the light house to Egypt Beach—another two hour patrol. These patrols were 24/7 with rotating crews.

"We also stood watch from the tower at the station, identified all ships and aircraft that we spotted, and kept a log of their movements. We had regular classes to attend, and did rescue work when needed. There were sixty-five men in all there. We stood watch with the lighthouse keeper at Minot Light. I was up there when a terrific storm hit. The waves seemed about seventy-five feet high and pounded away at the lighthouse, at times coming right up to the windows. We were trapped there for three days—to wait out the storm. I served in Scituate for a year—1942-'43."

After his Scituate service, Sieminski got orders to report to a Coast Guard School at Groton for a six months course in diesel engineering, maintenance and operation. From there he was sent back to Boston to join the U.S.S. *Sea Cloud*. It was, according to Sieminski, about a three hundred foot luxury yacht—a four-masted schooner, owned by the Hutton family, and loaned to the Coast Guard. A picture of the ship in its original configuration bears a striking resemblance to the U.S.S. *Eagle*, the white tall ship that serves as a Coast Guard training ship. But when Sieminski joined it, the ship had been converted for war patrols, including weather watch and anti-submarine duties.

"The masts and sails had been removed and she was powered by four huge Krupp diesels and two big generators. Guns had been added, as well as depth charges, including 'hedgehogs' [depth charges shot forward from the bow], and two rows of 'ash cans' [depth charges that rolled from the stern into the water]. Our area of operation was essentially the entire North Atlantic and some of the South Atlantic. Our home port was in Newfoundland, and we operated out of there for about thirty-five day patrols, returning to refuel and re-arm. A few times we spotted enemy submarines and reported their location to the nearby task force. The North Atlantic weather was rough, and yachts roll, so I did get seasick at first, but got over it. Once, I was down in the boiler room when I spotted a fire just breaking out. I grabbed a big pot of coffee and doused it before it

The USS *Sea Cloud* upon which John Sieminski served. Shown here in its pre-war configuration, before the masts and sails were removed, guns and depth charges added.

could spread. About half of the *Sea Cloud's* crew was African-Americans who did the same jobs we did." Sieminski served on the converted luxury yacht for a year—1943-'44. Then he was sent to an airbase in Greenland.

"I loved Greenland. I think the weather there is better than in Boston. We were stationed on an airbase and did rescue work for disabled planes that made crash landings. For a while, I was a chauffeur for an Admiral Rose there, and that was good duty. On our off-duty hours, some of us would ice skate, ski, and climb a nearby glacier. I spent a year in Greenland and returned to Boston in December 1945, and with the war over, was soon discharged as a Master Machinist Mate 3rd Class. Sieminski received the Victory Medal, the American Campaign Medal, the European-African-Middle Eastern Medal, and a letter from President Truman congratulating him on his service. He is one of eleven brothers, eight of whom served in the military services during World War II.

"I came back to Scituate, met Barbara Robisheau, and we got married in 1948," he said.

They raised four children who are now grown and all live nearby. They are grandparents of three. Sieminski took advantage of the G.I. Bill for further technical training; eventually, he owned a couple of gas stations in Scituate.

Sieminski and his wife were members of St. Francis Parish in Scituate, which closed, where he was on Parish Council, and his wife served as a Eucharistic Minister. John Siemenski passed last year and his widow, Babara, is now living in Scituate with family.

A TIME FOR WAR

Diesel Boats Forever

Louis "Lou" Vanderstreet

"OUR LAST PATROL OF WORLD WAR II ABOARD THE USS *Bluefish* was our best...," said Louis "Lou" Vanderstreet of Humarock/Scituate, but for Vanderstreet, getting to that time and place was a long and difficult journey filled with many hazards and the possibility of instant failure or instant death along the way.

"I joined the Navy in April of 1944. After four weeks of boot camp, I volunteered for submarine duty. The requirements were rigorous. When we arrived at initial Sub School in New London, Connecticut, we became members of 'Spritz's Navy,' named after a chief torpedo man who had served in World War I, and had been re-called as Chief-at-Arms in charge of the new volunteers' initiation into the sub school program. Spritz's job was to weed us out," said Vanderstreet.

According to Vanderstreet, while at "Spritz's Navy," the new volunteers underwent physical, psychiatric, aptitude, and other testing to determine their fitness for submarine duty. "One of the questions that took me by surprise was: 'Why do you want to serve on submarines?' I

Louis Vanderstreet

didn't have an answer," Vanderstreet said with a chuckle. Among other ordeals while in "Spritz's Navy" was the pressure chamber where the volunteers were subjected to an endurance test of whether they could withstand the pressure equivalent to being one hundred feet underwater. Another challenge was mastering the Momson Lung, a vest-like breathing apparatus placed on the chest. The aspiring submariners had to rise from the bottom of a one hundred foot water tank using this apparatus. Aside from the dangers and agony of the tests, failure in any one of them resulted in instant elimination from the program.

"Discipline was very strict, we were the last to eat, and when not in school or doing physical training, we were assigned to kitchen police (KP) and other unsavory duties," Vanderstreet said. Those who "graduated" from "Spritz's Navy" went on to sub school at New London. Those who failed were immediately sent to a pier in New York with hazardous duty of manning the guns on the merchant ships. There was about a fifty percent washout rate all along the way during Vanderstreet's training. "One thing that was drilled into us from day one was: 'There is room for almost anything in a submarine, but a mistake.'"

At sub school the training became more rigorous. "When we entered, each of us was issued a brown notebook for taking notes in class. On Friday we handed them to our instructor. If a student did not get his back on Monday, it meant he was washed out." It was during the last four weeks of this phase of the sixteen-week sub school training when the students first went to sea in submarines. "These were World War I 'O'-class boats. They were very uncomfortable, and leaked, and this is where those who had claustrophobia, but didn't know it, washed themselves out." The sub school curriculum required every student to learn all the systems—hydraulics, fuel, air valves, torpedo tubes, etc., of the boat. There was a final drill where an officer walked with the student though the boat testing him on his knowledge on all of these complex systems. Upon completion of sub school, the graduates boarded a train for the West Coast and on to four more weeks of training at the advanced sub school in San Diego, California. Then Vanderstreet traveled to Mare Island near San Francisco, where he learned that he had been assigned to the U.S.S. *Bluefish*.

According to Vanderstreet, the *Bluefish* had an outstanding war record and was manned by the men who had sailed her through the war. "I was just a lowly seaman when I joined the group. I was initially assigned mess duties and given a 'hot bunk,' which meant I could use it if no one else was. We sailed under the Golden Gate Bridge headed for Pearl Harbor. Along the way we were subjected to countless diving drills. One time someone made a mistake in coordination, and in a surfacing drill, the diesel engines started before the main induction valve had been opened. It was chaotic. The engines sucked the air out of the sub. Things were flying around, men screaming, and one man was injured.

"I made three war patrols in the *Bluefish*," said Vanderstreet who during this phase was relieved of mess duty and raised in rank to operate air and surface radar as a Radio Man 3rd Class. "On my first war patrol, we had a running gun battle with a Japanese picket boat. We were on the surface. We sunk her. During all my patrols, the Japanese were notorious for laying floating mines, outlawed by the Geneva Convention. We traveled most of the time on the surface and these mines were invisible unless visual conditions were perfect. If a submarine hit one of these mines, the boat sinks immediately. The only time we could relax was when we were submerged. We also performed 'lifeguard duty,' that is picking up downed fliers. We picked up three one day, but the pilot who stayed with the plane so his men could bail out, was so badly injured he died on board the *Bluefish*. We buried him at sea. He was awarded the Navy Cross." Vanderstreet recalled one of the hazards of lifeguard duty was being exposed to enemy shore batteries and enemy aircraft, and often in shallow water, so "we could not dive." Overall the submarines saved five hundred and four downed airmen.

"At sea we had no friends," he said. "A submarine's greatest threat is another submarine. On my last war patrol we spotted a Japanese submarine before she spotted us and we torpedoed her. We could read their code and we knew it was one of Japan's largest submarines, carrying 10,000 gallons of aviation gasoline and a German prototype jet engine. At dawn we picked up three survivors and they became prisoners-of-war. We treated them well."

Vanderstreet mustered out about six months after the war ended and joined the Brockton Fire Department, but the Navy was not quite through with him. He was recalled to active duty in 1950. After being released from the Navy, Vanderstreet went back to his job at the Brockton Fire Department. He married Phyllis Yesonis in 1954; they have one son, Louis Charles, who lives in Vermont. During his twenty-six years with the Brockton Fire Department, he rose to the rank of captain. He was seriously injured in the line of duty in 1976, and retired.

Among Vanderstreet's many military citations and awards are the coveted Dolphin Badge, Submarine Combat pin with two Stars, Asiatic Pacific Campaign Medal with four Stars, Philippine Liberation Medal with one star, the Philippine Government Combat Ribbon, the Meritorious Defense Medal, and a World War II Victory Medal. He is a member of Scituate's American Legion Post #144.

A TIME FOR WAR

Haley's War

George Haley

G EORGE HALEY SCANNED THE CRUEL SEA AHEAD from
the deck of the Coast Guard Cutter *Duane* making
full speed to the location of the submarine that had been
detected shadowing the task force. It was a cold April
17th, 1943, during the Battle of the Atlantic. The *Duane*
was part of a task unit, which includeded the *Spencer*
as flagship and four British escorts. The task unit was
providing escort for convoy HX-233 comprised of fifty-
six ships. About 500 nautical miles southwest of Ireland
one of the merchantmen was torpedoed. Sonar on both
the *Spencer* and the *Duane* picked up the submarine's
location.

"After graduating from high school, and about a
month after the Japanese attack on Pearl Harbor, I joined
the Coast Guard on January 2, 1942," said George Haley,
lifelong resident of Cohasset. "I was sworn in at
Boston. I did not go to boot camp. They wanted a typist
and I had typed at school. So they put me right into an
office in Boston in the Custom House." Seeking action
outside the typing pool, Haley joined the crew of the

The USS *Duane* lays a barrage of depth charges over the U-175, a German U-boat in the North Atlantic, 1943.

Duane and sailed for convoy escort duty in March 1943.

"The *Spencer* depth charged it first. They damaged the submarine. We teamed with them in the hunt, but we already had contact on our sonar," Haley said. "When we laid our barrage, the submarine was still submerged. We laid down a pattern of depth charges to a depth of fifty or a hundred feet, and we swung around in a circle scanning the surface."

Haley remembers spotting the black conning tower of the submarine break the surface of the cold gray sea ahead of the *Duane*. "As we closed in, we were firing five-inch and three-inch guns and twenty millimeter canons at the surfacing sub," Haley recalls. "I could see a German sailor come up on the deck of the sub to fire at us from its main deck gun. The sailor disappeared in a hail of twenty millimeter rounds."

The conning tower of the sub was smoking, Haley recalls, and the submarine was moving ahead slowly, circling to the right. Haley watched as the submarine began sinking by the stern just as the boarding party's lifeboat from the *Spencer* reached it. He is one of the few remaining eyewitnesses to "the first Americans to board an enemy man-of-war at sea since the War of 1812." Before the sub went down, the boarding party was able to identify it as the U-175.

"As the submarine was sinking, its crewmen started jumping overboard. They wore life jackets. And we could see their heads bobbing in the cold water. We lowered a boat and picked up survivors. We helped them board and we took good care of them. We gave them blankets and coffee. We had a brig below and we put them there."

Navy records report that one German officer and eighteen men were rescued by the *Spencer* and twenty-two others by the *Duane*. U-175s commanding officer was killed in the initial surface gunfire. According to Time Life's *The Battle of the Atlantic*, U-boat Captain Gerhardt Muntz and six of his crew died on the U-175s

German sailors from U-175 climb up the ropes from the USS *Duane's* lifeboat.

deck as a result of the barrage. The rest of the U-boat's crew escaped as their ship sank.

The battle had been won, but Haley's war was not over. He returned to Norfolk, Virginia, where the *Duane* was prepared to participate in the invasion of southern France. "We had finished our North Atlantic escort duty, and at Norfolk Navy Yard, the ship was fitted out with communications equipment. From there we shipped out as part of the Eighth Amphibious Force. We sailed to Naples where we trained another three months. The Luftwaffe identified our ship as an important target. They followed us from Gibraltar. Each night they would fly over Naples harbor dropping illumination flares and try to bomb us.

George Haley (*right*) escorts a German submarine officer to the captain of the USS *Duane.*

From Naples we sailed to participate in the invasion of southern France on August 15, 1944."

Following duty during the invasion of southern France, the *Duane* provided Mediterranean escort duties. Haley achieved the rank of Seaman First Class. For his service he was awarded three citations, including for action in sinking the U-175, and for participating in the invasion of southern France. He received two campaign ribbons with three bronze battle stars.

After being mustered out of the Navy at the end of World War II, Haley spent many years with the Post Office in Cohasset. Following his retirement, Haley operated his own business—"Cohasset Locksmith."

Hell on Wheels

Charles "Charlie" Snell

A NYONE WHO ATTENDED LAST MEMORIAL DAY ceremonies on the Common in Scituate would have seen him. He wore his World War II brown Army uniform with the distinctive "Eisenhower jacket." On his left shoulder was sewn his Technical Sergeant stripes and one of the most storied combat patches of World War II, a triangle depicting tank treads crossed with a lightning bolt and the words, "Hell on Wheels."

Charles "Charlie" Snell was escorted to a folding chair on the grass to the side of the memorial. In his remarks Representative James Cantwell made special recognition of Snell as a man who had served with General George Patton. Following the ceremony children from the elementary schools surrounded Snell to hand him their handmade cards honoring veterans. Junior and senior high school students, and adults, wanted to meet this veteran and thank him for his service.

Snell, a long-time resident of Scituate, was one of a family of ten brothers and sisters. As a child and young adult he dug clams near Hull to help out the family. "We would dig 'em to eat or sell."

Charley Snell poses in front of a Sherman tank just like "Faith Family" at Fort Devins, Massachusetts just before mustering out circa July 1945. Charley is since deceased.

In the fall of 1943, just after his eighteenth birthday Snell got an unexpected surprise. "The Army came looking for me in a jeep. I had been drafted." Shortly after being sent to Fort Knox, Kentucky, for Infantry basic training, Snell was switched to training for the Tank Corps. "There were five positions in the [Sherman] tank, and we were trained on all five so we could take over in an emergency. The positions were driver, assistant driver, gunner, loader, and tank commander. I was the tank driver." According to Snell, five men in the confined space of a Sherman tank was a pretty crowded environment.

Following training Snell shipped out with his unit to England as Company F, 2nd Armored Division, 66th Armored Regiment. Once there Snell's unit "picked up" a tank and were loaded on an LST (Landing Ship Tank) for shipment to France as part of the invasion. Snell and his tank landed on Omaha Beach in Normandy on D-day plus 3, June 9, 1944. It was from there that Snell's Division earned its nickname, "Hell on Wheels," as they raced across France with the rest of the Third Army during July and August.

But Hell on Wheels goes both ways. "The tanks were hot in the summer and cold in the winter. We were in the tank most of the time. We just kept moving night and day, and we kept to the main roads, and when we first came upon a bridge one of the tanks ahead of us started across and fell through. After that we were ordered 'no more crossing bridges on the road—go down the bank of the rivers, cross the rivers and come back up the other bank to get back on the road.' We could go through three to five feet of water."

Snell recalls the top speed of the Sherman tank was "twenty-eight miles per hour and along the way there was shelling and all that stuff going on. They used to deliver the gas by truck and we would use five gallon containers to fill her up. It took two men—one to pour and one standing by with a fire extinguisher. We only got about two miles on a gallon and the tank had a two hundred gallon tank."

Ergonomic considerations that we take for granted now did not exist then. "The tank had a Wright radial air cooled [airplane] engine. And when you were inside with the engine going and the hatches open, the suction of the outside air practically sucked the clothes off your body. We were sitting on the engine and it was so loud—as was the cannon. We closed the hatch to fire the cannon in the turret. When we fired the 75 mm cannon, the tank would roll back about a foot, the breach of the cannon would open inside and the red hot thirty-nine pound shell was ejected upon us. We had helmets with earphones. Most of the time we kept the German infantry running from us. Our targets were also German tanks. At night we were sometimes attacked by German planes. I ran over a mine one time and it blew off the track, but we fixed it."

Every unit named its tank, but there was one caveat, the name had to begin with the letter designating each unit's Company. "We named our tank 'Faith Family,' after our faith and families and it brought us through the war."

Snell's Division reached the Albert Canal in Belgium on September 8, 1944, crossed the German border on September 18, 1944, and on October 3, 1944, attacked the Siegfried Line, and breached it. In December 1944, the Division was ordered to help contain the German Ardennes offensive, the Battle of the Bulge. During the Battle of the Bulge, Hell on Wheels fought in eastern Belgium, blunting the German penetration of American lines. The Division fought in the Ardennes forest in deep snow and arctic conditions. "Somewhere we rescued some paratroopers, and I got frostbite," Snell said.

On April 11, 1945, Snell was with the first American Division to reach the Elbe River. "We crossed the Elbe at night." In July, Snell's Division was the first American unit to enter the German capital city of Berlin. For his service Snell was awarded many decorations including the Belgian Fourraguerre, Distinguished Unit Badge, and Campaign and Victory medals.

Snell served eighteen months in "Faith Family" following Patton from Normandy to Berlin. A large map depicting his grand campaign hangs on his living room wall. After the war he married Louise Jackman of Norwell and they raised four children—one son and three daughters—in Scituate. Married fifty-four years, and now a widower, Snell has thirteen grandchildren. He had a long career in the motor repair business. He retired from the town of Scituate as Chief Operator of the Scituate Water plant.

A TIME FOR WAR

Survivors

Irene Jacobson

"I HAVE A FAMILY MEMBERSHIP IN VETERANS' organizations and I address veterans groups that have dubbed me the 'youngest survivor of the bombing of Pearl Harbor,'" said Dr. Leilani Doty, Ph.D., a neuropsychologist on the faculty of the University of Florida, who was visiting her mother, Irene Jacobson, a resident at Life Care Nursing home on the Driftway in Scituate. Doty, Jacobson's oldest daughter, provided support in recalling her mother's harrowing story. It is simply the story of one young couple caught in the crosshairs of the target of the Japanese surprise attack on the U.S. Navy fleet at Pearl Harbor on December 7, 1941.

"I was born in New York City—the Bronx," Jacobson said. The family moved to Massachusetts and she grew up in Everett. "My husband, John [Peter] Jacobson was a sergeant in the Army. I called him Peter." The couple married in Cambridge in 1938. In 1940, Peter was assigned to new duty as a master sergeant in transportation attached to the U.S. Army's Coastal Artillery near Honolulu, Hawaii. "We lived in the married quarters of

Doctor Leilani Doty (*right*), with her mother,
the late Irene Jacobson, a resident at Scituate
Life Care nursing home in Scituate.

Schofield Barracks not far from Honolulu." While living
at the barracks, the dependents participated in drills that
included leaving the house to run to foxholes in the
backyards of the barracks quarters.

On December 7th, a Sunday morning, "We were in our
quarters at the Schofield Army barracks. My husband and
I were reading the newspaper, having toast and coffee
when we heard loud noises. At first we thought it was
military maneuvers," she said. At that time Jacobson was
two months pregnant with her first child.

"A soldier who had served in the last war ran down in
front of the barracks shouting, 'This is war!'" Jacobson

said. "We, the women and children, ran to the foxholes, and the men left to join their units. My husband was in charge of trucks and he sent men to their units located at different places along the coast. Other trucks came and picked us up to take us to a school." The school was located about thirty miles away from the barracks and the civilian military dependents stayed there for about six weeks.

"While there we did what we were told," Jacobson said. "Each day they posted a casualty list," in a prominent place for all to see. Jacobson still recalls the grim sight of trucks of body bags passing by on the road.

After six weeks at the school, the civilian military dependents were returned to Schofield Barracks, and then Jacobson went to work for the Post Office to help out.

"They told us they wanted to get us out—women and children first," Jacobson said.

In the dark days following the attack, the military leaders had ordered as a high priority on a long list of needs for men and equipment, the evacuation of families of military personnel from Hawaii to the continental United States to begin as soon as it was feasible.

It took four months until April 1942 for Jacobson to be evacuated.

"We evacuated on a [converted] troop ship…the *Aquitania,* that sailed from Australia to pick up the dependents." According to the record, the *Aquitania*, a British luxury liner launched in 1913, served in both World Wars. During its military service it was converted to a troop ship. In early 1942, the *Aquitania* sailed from Australia unescorted through submarine infested waters to attempt the daring rescue.

"We were only allowed one suitcase. It was a beautiful ship. We had to make do with the food that was on the ship." The *Aquitania* sailed for the West Coast of the United States protected by an escort. At the time, Japanese submarines had been sighted in the waters not far from Pearl Harbor. "It took us six days to reach the West Coast. The Red Cross met us at our destination— San Pedro, California. From there I boarded a train bound for Chicago and then on to Boston. It took four days and three nights. My parents and family in Everett did not know if I was dead or alive, or that I was pregnant. I arrived in South Station, took the subway and then a bus to Everett. I got off the bus. I walked to my mother's house. When my father heard I was home safe, he closed his grocery store and came home for the happy reunion."

When it came time, the Army granted her husband leave to come home and be with her for the birth of their first child.

Her husband Peter served in World War II and Korea. He died in 1973 of a heart attack. Jacobson has three daughters, eight grandchildren, and eight great grandchildren.

"I like history and economics," Jacobson said. "I wish my grandchildren wisdom and strength, and I tell them knowledge is power."

Liberator Pilot

Joe Clapp

"JOE, YOU WILL HAVE TO PUSH ME OUT!"

Joseph "Joe" E. Clapp recalled the prophetic words of Jack Buckler, his friend, mentor, and pilot in command of his four-engine B-24 Liberator Bomber. It was late in their training days in the States and the two were discussing the possibility of being shot down on a mission and having to parachute.

Before Clapp had obtained the right to sit in the coveted co-pilot seat of a B-24, he had to endure many—at times seemingly impossible—trials.

"My stint in flying began when I used to work during summer breaks piling lumber at the Welsh Company in Scituate," Clapp, a life-long resident of Scituate said of his days at Scituate High School. "Little by little I would put a few dollars aside" for flying lessons out of Hanover.

Clapp went to work for Works Progress Association (WPA) when he graduated from Scituate High School in1939. "Then you couldn't join the Army Air Corps

Joe Clapp in the cockpit of his B-24.

unless you had two years of college, but I saw an ad in the newspapers that if you could pass an exam equivalent to two years of college you could get in. So I went to Boston. I thought it was probably a waste of time, but I passed with a score of ninety-seven. That very day I was sworn in and given two weeks to report to a Captain Newman at Fort Devens." Clapp arrived and told the sergeant that he was to report to a Captain Newman. The sergeant had other ideas and put Clapp to work washing pots and pans. "I had been on Kitchen Police [K.P.] for two days when two Military Policemen came into the mess hall asking why I did not report to Captain Newman as ordered." After being marched under guard to the Captain's office, Clapp reported, "I explained that the sergeant wouldn't listen to me, and neither would those in charge of K.P."

Clapp was issued a new set of uniforms as an air cadet, and assigned new barracks. From basic training, Clapp went to Michigan State College to complete two years of college in three months. "From there we were sent to primary flight training in Corsicana, Texas for three months," Clapp said. "We trained in the PT-19 [Primary Trainer], a single-wing open cockpit airplane. It was a beautiful plane, and flying it was a lot of fun.

"From Primary training we went on to Majors Field located near Dallas at Greenville, Texas for Basic Flight training where we flew BT-13s, which was a more advance trainer with a powerful engine. They called the BT-13, [manufactured by the Vultee Company] the 'Vultee Vibrator.' At Majors Field they divided us up into squadrons. We flew with instructors and practiced formation flying, navigation, and instrument flying. I was then assigned to multi-engine school and went to Ellington Field in Texas. Once we graduated, we were made Flight Officers. I was assigned to be a P-38 fighter pilot, and we waited for our slots at the P-38 school in California. I wanted to get into the war, and word came down that if you could pass the test you could get into the war quicker by flying the B-24 Liberator Bomber."

Soon Clapp was on his way to Charleston, South Carolina, to meet his new crew and his new B-24. "My pilot was Jack Buckler," he said.

More training followed and soon Clapp and his crew were winging their way to Mitchell Field in New York. Once there, Clapp called his girlfriend, Noreen Keefe, an Army nurse lieutenant, and her mother to come and visit.

Soon orders came down for deployment to Italy. "We were flying at night across the ocean at thirteen thousand feet, and ice started building up on the wing. We turned on the deicers and suddenly the lights went out!" Without electricity there was no instrumentation and neither Buckler nor Clapp knew if they were diving or climbing, when suddenly the ocean appeared. They were headed straight for it when the power went back on. They recovered at about five hundred feet above the surface.

"We operated as part of the 15th Air Force, 456th Bomb Group out of Cerignola in South East Italy," said Clapp. But before we were scheduled to fly as a crew, they broke us up for five missions. On the third of these missions Jack Buckler's plane was shot down and crashed." Clapp asked the retuning crews how many chutes they saw—the answer was nine. There should have been ten. "I knew right then it was Jack," Clapp said. "Later when the pilot of Jack's ship, Rosie Rosenberg, made it back to the base I asked about Jack. The last he saw was Buckler standing in the open bomb bay; later they found Buckler dead on the ground."

Clapp went on to serve with distinction, accumulating roughly twenty-four missions over central and eastern Europe. To paraphrase Clapp, who also once flew a B-17—flying the B-17 was like driving a Cadillac, flying the B-24 was like driving a five-ton Army truck. "You were working all the time," he added. At the war's end, Clapp piloted from Italy to Bradley Field, Connecticut, in one of one hundred and nineteen B-24s as part of a huge formation. He returned to Scituate to become a builder. He married Noreen Keefe and had four children, three daughters and a son, six grandchildren, and eight great grandchildren. Noreen passed in 1995. Clapp then married Patricia McGinnis who passed in 1999.

A TIME FOR WAR

Glider Pilot

John Coe

JOHN COE, A LONG TIME RESIDENT OF COHASSET, was born in Medford, Massachusetts, in 1921. His family moved to New Jersey where he spent his early years. Later he returned to Massachusetts where he attended the Lenox School, in Lenox, Massachusetts.

When Coe graduated from high school in 1942, the world was at war. He worked for a period after graduation as a proofreader in New Jersey. While working there he enlisted in the Army on January 28, 1943.

"I wanted to be a paratrooper but after basic training the processing officer looked at me and said, 'You are too skinny.'" According to Army records, Coe was 6' 2" and 155 pounds at that time.

"But they are looking now for glider pilots," the processing officer told him.

Coe qualified for training at the First Allied Airborne School—Advanced Glider School at Dalhart, Texas.

"We started out training as pilots in small single-engine airplanes and then we moved on to flying

Glider pilot John Coe, at a base somewhere
in England during World War II.

twin-engine aircraft." According to Coe the training in
powered aircraft was specifically for the purpose of
transitioning to glider pilot. Coe was commissioned as a
Flight Officer upon graduation from Advanced Glider
School.

Coe's Stateside training lasted a total of six months and
fifteen days. He would spend the next two years, five
months and three days serving in Africa and Europe until
war's end.

On May 13, 1943, Coe and his group shipped out for North Africa. In his book, *On Wings of Troop Carriers in World War II,* author Robert E. Callahan includes "Flt O John W. Coe" in his list of the 50th Troop Carrier Squadron personnel on board the U.S.S. *West Point* to Africa."

The first use of gliders by the Army in combat operations was the invasion of Sicily in July of 1943. A combination of navigational errors, inexperience, friendly fire from ships, and high winds played havoc on the initial part of the operation. Less than half of the 137 gliders involved got to their landing zones. Many landed in the sea with a total loss of 605 personnel. The disaster was one of the worst of the war leading the Supreme Allied Commander, General Eisenhower, to want to scrap using airborne troops altogether. However, other generals persuaded him to change his mind allowing the invasion to continue. Coe would be part of that as a lone pilot of a cargo glider.

"From North Africa we were towed by a C-47 across the Mediterranean to Sicily, landing near Salerno. The gliders were designed to come in a day or two after the paratroopers. We would bring in jeeps, howitzers, and supplies. And in one invasion we brought in troops."

The airborne component of the D-Day invasion was called "Operation Neptune." Coe was selected to fly his glider across the English Channel to France on the fourth day of the invasion in support of the 82nd and 101st airborne troops that preceded him. During these operations the gliders, according to an eyewitness, "did not actually land but crashed more or less successfully."

After D-Day the gliders continued to support the troops as they moved through France. By August 15, 1944, Coe was in support of the airborne units in southern France in "Operation Dragoon." He recalls a very hard landing there while carrying thirteen troops.

"The wind was bad and I crashed into a tree. I was a mess. Blood all over the place. I was the only one hurt. I was stumbling around and one of the troops was surprised. When he saw me, he said, 'We thought you were dead.' The troops were okay and they got me to a first aid station, but it was full of injured paratroopers so I was evacuated to Gibraltar. I ended up in the hospital in England and after convalescing I went back to flying the glider."

Readers familiar with the book *A Bridge too Far*, or the film version, know that the story is based on the Allied "Operation Market Garden," the ill-fated invasion of German-occupied Holland that took place in September 1944, and its disastrous consequences. Coe participated in that campaign flying a glider being towed from England.

"I was shot at over the Channel, but I was lucky I made a good landing there [Holland], near Eindhoven," Coe said. An unknown soldier writing in an online blog, "Riviera Ramblings," relates what happened next: "John W. Coe and I had planned to get in on the fighting, so when I learned of the coming attack I picked up Coe at the aid station...As we neared the town we started climbing a hill that had a walled cemetery on its crest. Someone from behind yelled 'down' and we hit the dirt—we were caught in a crossfire from machine guns. A lot of calls for medics here. Crossfire very effective...we were pinned down...bullets were buzzing around like a swarm of bees..."

Having survived the landing and German attack they met people of the occupied country. "The Dutch were so glad to see us," Coe said. Not long after that Coe was evacuated from Holland and returned to England.

But Coe's war was not over. He participated in Operation Varsity, which was the crossing of the Rhine in March 1945.

Coe received many citations and awards for his service. He was discharged as a first lieutenant. Of his service he said: "I enjoyed every minute flying the glider."

Following the war, Coe went to Lafayette College in eastern Pennsylvania on the GI Bill, graduating in 1949 with a degree in English. He worked as a salesman for Remington Rand and later had his own business as a manufacturers' representative.

He and his wife Marcia live in Cohasset. They have a son, Charles, Jr., a lieutenant colonel serving in Korea as an Army optometrist, and a daughter, Mary Connolly, who lives in California with her husband, Joe, their three children, and one grandchild.

"I had two lucky things in my life," Coe said, "I made it through the war and I met and married Marcia."

A TIME FOR WAR

Letter from Okinawa

Anthony Ferreira

T HE BATTLE OF OKINAWA, JAPAN'S LAST MAJOR island fortress just three hundred and fifty miles from the homeland, began on Easter Sunday 1945. The battle resulted in 50,000 American soldiers, sailors, airmen, and Marine casualties, and untold numbers of Japanese deaths and wounded. The Japanese were dug into the ground and holed up in caves on the volcanic ridge lined island fortress in a "back to the door—no holds barred" struggle to defend their homeland. The U.S. victory there was achieved by what one U.S. general called "the blowtorch and corkscrew" method.

What follows is a heretofore unpublished letter of a Scituate Marine—now deceased—who served there, Corporal Anthony "Bud" Ferreira. Former two-term Scituate Selectman Evelyn Ferreira, his widow, lovingly preserved the letter over the years. It reads as follows:

I enlisted in the Marine Corps September 4, 1942, and was discharged October 19, 1945. During that time I was a BAR (Browning automatic rifle) man with G. Co. 2nd Battalion, 5th Marines, 1st Marine Division at Pelelui.

A TIME FOR WAR

History records the Battle of Pelelui took place during September and November 1944 on the Pacific island of Pelelui. The U.S. Forces, originally consisting of only the 1st Marine Division and later by the Army's 81st Division fought to capture an airstrip on the small coral island. The battle remains one of the most controversial of World War II due to its questionable strategic value and high death toll. When considering the number of men involved, Pelelui had the highest casualty rate of any battle in the Pacific War.

I ended up a squad leader on Okinawa at place called Kunishi Ridge. I had just gotten back to my unit from the (field) hospital from a previous wound. The doctor had patched me up, but in fact the wound had not fully healed. ...The Top Sergeant asked me if I wanted to go with the squad, (which had been reorganized since my injury with a new) squad leader. It was too late to change the newly appointed squad leader and I agreed to go along.

After the bombarding of the ridge (where the Japanese were dug in) and with the support of tanks, we got up on the ridge. I helped the squad leader place the men. The Japs started dropping in grenades (from above) until all the men were hit, but the squad leader and myself. We had no alternative but to get the men off the ridge. While they were going down the ridge, the squad leader was beside me when a grenade landed at my feet. I thought of kicking it over the ridge, but I couldn't as the wounded men were moving off below. I yelled for them to run, and the squad leader to roll over on his stomach. Then I rolled over on the top of him, taking the full blunt, as the grenade went off.

Photo from *The Old Breed: A History of the First Marine Division in World War II* by George McMillan shows Marines marching in Okinawa on the day World War II ended in Europe. Anthony Ferreira is the third man on the left in the column moving toward the front lines.

When I recovered my senses to a certain degree of consciousness, but in a dazed condition, I asked the squad leader if he was okay and he said he was. I told him to take off down the ridge while I covered him. After he got down, I followed. Below the ridge we were pinned down with everything dropping in on us— mortar, artillery, etc. The men were getting wounded again. I went into semi-consciousness, and I could hear the squad leader talking to me, but I couldn't seem to do anything. I finally snapped out of it, and he asked me to take the wounded back to the C.P. (Command Post). I suggested that he go, and I stay because I didn't even feel like moving. He said he should stay because he was the squad leader.

I asked the men to follow me, but they didn't want to because the fire power was so heavy. So I had to figure out something. About a hundred yards away, there was a tank shelling between two ridges. I asked the men if I got the tank for cover would they go back then, and they agreed. I proceeded to the tank under heavy fire...I made it to the tank...I told the tank commander of the situation over the phone (the phone that was attached to the tank for infantry to communicate with the tank commander) and requested that he bring the tank over for cover while I got the wounded out.

This was done, and I got them back safely, where the corpsmen took over. About that time I had it and I flopped. One of the corpsmen came to my side, and said that I should go to the hospital. I told him I would be all right. The Company Commander, Lt. Breene, ordered me taken to the hospital. The fire power was so thick we had to be taken out by tank and then by plane...

Semper fidelis,

Anthony J. Ferreira

For his wounds received in combat that day, Ferreira was awarded a Purple Heart. For his actions that day, Ferreira received no awards for valor, except the life-long satisfaction from the awareness that his actions had saved the lives of many of the men in his squad. For his family his letter is a legacy that he is numbered among those who served in a manner, and at a place and time, where "uncommon valor was a common virtue."

"Melanesian Nightmare"

George Hause

O VERSHADOWED BY OTHER PERHAPS MORE spectacular campaigns such as Tarawa, Guadalcanal, and Iwo Jima in the Pacific during World War II, the long struggle of the U.S. forces in New Guinea is often relegated to a footnote in history—remembered mostly by those who served in what was dubbed the "Melanesian Nightmare." George Hause of Scituate is one of those who remembers.

"We arrived from Australia not long after the battle of Buna ended in January 1943," Hause said. "There was an airstrip in the Buna area from which the Japanese were ousted after almost a year of nasty jungle fighting by the infantry—both ours and Aussies. The battle of Buna was the beginning of General Mac Arthur's leap-frog strategy.

"In May 1943 we loaded on LSTs and moved to the north side of the island to Doba Dura. There were two big airstrips there. I was one of the welders. We put down Summerfield matting, a metal surface over dirt, so our planes could land. During that period we were bombed at lot, but we kept working. The raids were

George Hause somewhere in the jungles of Melanesia.

mostly at night. During the day we looked up and saw our P-38s shooting down the Japanese bombers. We were cheering like at a football game. We staged there. It was very hot. I had malaria a couple of times. My eyes got yellow."

Following the construction of the air base, Hause's group of Army engineers was ordered to load their equipment back on the LSTs and to go up the North coast of the world's second largest island with the 32nd Infantry Division. "We sailed up the coast of New Guinea on these small amphibious transports to a place called Saidor, which was occupied by the Japanese. The Japanese must have seen us coming because they retreated into the bush and high cliffs overlooking the beach. The infantry rushed into the steaming jungle, but we could not get our equipment in quickly from the LSTs. The Japanese were up in caves in the cliffs shooting down on us. It was a natural fortress. We were outnumbered with five thousand Japanese troops sitting on the high ground."

Once ashore and into the malaria infested jungle other problems soon materialized. "There was no water. My company was to take the water hole. It took fifteen days to capture the well. The rumor was that we weren't going to push the Japanese out, but we were going to move in with them. The plan was to cut off the Japanese supply lines. We were on River Defense. The river was a natural barrier. It came out of the mountains and flowed down to the sea. We marched up the river from the mouth. We guarded one side; the Japanese were on the other side. I was manning a .50 caliber machine gun.

"We built a PT boat base near Saidor. One of my pals knew a skipper of a PT boat and he took me down to introduce me. The skipper was Paul Fay. He had been a classmate of Jack Kennedy at Harvard. He would later become the Secretary of the Navy. The PT boats would patrol off Wewak at night to make sure the Japanese did not try to invade. So we were blocking the river and the Navy was blocking the ocean."

After a while Hause's group was relieved, but not for long.

"We loaded back on LSTs, and travelled several days north of Saidor to the Island of Biak," Hause said. According to the record, the fighting there was fierce over a crucial objective—the reopening of the Mokmer Air Field. The American Army lost 435 killed, and 2,360 wounded. The Japanese killed are estimated at 6,125, with 460 taken prisoner. "We liberated the Island and freed hundreds of captive Formosans who were like Japanese slaves. It took several weeks," Hause said. The Battle of Biak was the practical end of the New Guinea campaign and this opened the door to the Philippines. "We went on to land at Leyte, and went all the way to Manila. We were ready to go to Japan when Harry [President Truman] dropped the bomb."

Prior to his experiences in New Guinea, Hause said, "I went to Mechanic Arts High School in Boston, where the Prudential Building now sits. I lived in Roslindale. In June of 1942, I went to Boston to join the Marine Corps but because I had burned my foot welding, they turned me down. Two weeks later I was drafted into the Army. The Army didn't discriminate; they took me burn or no burn." He added that following months of arduous training, "in March 1943, we went over on a 10,000 man troop ship to Sidney, Australia."

Hause met Mary Quinn in Roslindale. They were married in 1951, and raised three children and have five grandchildren. Hause retired from a long career with the Department of Defense. He was one of the founders of the government workers union, NAGE. Hause lobbied the Massachusetts delegation in Washington and got to know Congressman John F. Kennedy. Later President Kennedy appointed Hause to the "Health Insurance through Social Security Committee," precursor to Medicare, on May 20, 1962. Hause also worked with

Ted Kennedy in serving on the committee. Hause proudly wears a PT 109 pin.

For his service, Hause was awarded, among other things, four battle stars, the Philippine Liberation Medal, and was cited for bravery under fire. He served mostly in combat without home leave for three and one half years.

"I am proud to have fought for my country," Hause said.

A TIME FOR WAR

Military Policeman

Dominic Bonanno

T HE COARSE WOOL ARMY JACKET, MORE BROWN than olive, hangs silhouetted against the white wall of the narrow hallway. The corporal stripes, the combat hash marks on the sleeves—once bright gold—and the formerly vibrantly colored ribbons and awards sewn on the tunic have, chameleon-like, faded into the dark color of the uniform. To the right of the jacket pinned to the wall is a large American flag. Directly across on the opposite wall hangs a framed ancient black and white photograph of his father in his World War I Army field attire looking—as if with pride—across at his son's uniform; all items lovingly put on display in the home by the World War II veteran's "keeper of the flame" daughter. Old albums of photographs are brought out filled with pictures of young G.I.s at the front smiling in "harm's way"—a "band of brothers" from another era. A rapidly diminishing and irreplaceable precious resource. Photos fade but some memories are still bright as if it were yesterday....

Sergeant Joseph Bonanno holding two pistols outside the wire of a temporary POW camp in Germany during the final Allied drive into Germany.

"We were guarding prisoners at the front in Germany close to the Russian lines, not long after the Battle of the Bulge. Suddenly we look up to see truckloads of Germans coming right at us down the road," said Dominic "Dom" Bonanno, originally from South Boston, but a long time resident of Scituate. "We didn't know. We thought we were being attacked so we went into top alert. And then we could see they weren't armed or anything, but they were trying to get away from the Russians. It was a very funny thing, looking back, they were trying to get into our stockade on their own."

Bonanno and his unit of Military Police followed the Army as it moved across Europe, from D-Day until the end of the war. "We'd keep moving up to the front as it advanced. Often we would bivouac in bombed out buildings at the front as we moved. Our job was to guard the prisoners and get them squared away; for example, we had to make sure they were deloused. We treated the prisoners well. I think they were glad to be captured by us."

Our troops were taking so many prisoners and it was the responsibility of Bonanno and his special detachment of military police to guard them until relieved. The prisoners were herded into quickly erected prison camps, little more than barbed wire fenced areas with guard towers. But as the front moved forward though France, Belgium, Holland, and Germany, new camps would be hastily constructed as more prisoners were taken. Bonanno and his men would always be on the advance as the front moved forward. They were the first unit to take control of the captured Germans.

"It was bad—especially at night—bombs were going off all around," he said. Once the stockades were up, the prisoners would be incarcerated and under the military police guard until they could be trucked back to the rear, according to Bonanno.

"We could patrol the perimeter of the stockade in pairs only during the day," he said. But since Bonanno and his unit were always so close to the action, they never knew if elements of the German Army would try a surprise rescue. "We manned the guard towers at night with the machine guns." As soon as the prisoners were shipped out, Bonanno's unit would move forward to the front to take custody of the prisoners in a newly cobbled prison camp.

"We kept guarding prisoners even after the hostilities ended, but our sergeant said to us, 'Don't get excited, you are going to the Pacific Theatre.' But that's when it was decided to drop the atomic bomb [on Hiroshima] and the war in the Pacific ended as well," said Bonanno.

Bonanno, who graduated from Charlestown High School in 1942, sailed to Europe on the *Queen Elizabeth,* which had been converted to a military transport. "I came home on a little boat called the *Marine Raven*, a small ship, and we arrived in New York. When I got back to the States, they gave us a thirty day furlough, later extended, and that is when Frances Guarnotta and I married. My wife and I were high school sweethearts," said Bonanno. "She wrote to me almost every day, but I didn't get the letters every day, and she waited for me to get back. We married two weeks after I got back to the States on December 16, 1945."

Bonanno served on active duty, from April 1943, and in combat from D-Day, June 6th, 1944, until the end of the war in Europe in 1945— a little over twenty months. He was honorably discharged on December 10, 1945.

The Bonannos have one son, three daughters, and eight grandchildren. Bonanno went to college on the G.I. Bill, graduating from Boston Teachers College in 1952. Bonanno spent his career as a teacher, including thirty-two years teaching industrial arts in Scituate at the Gates School. He retired as a teacher from Scituate Public Schools in 1987.

"I was assigned to the 620th Military Police Escort Guard Company. Our unit was awarded two battle stars;

one, I remember, was for the Battle of the Bulge. I was not a hero in the war, but I am proud to be registered in the World War II Memorial in Washington."

A TIME FOR WAR

A Life of Service at Sea

Myron Boluch

"Everybody in my Amherst class wanted to be a Navy pilot and I went to Springfield to take the pre-flight physical but I flunked the eye test," said Myron Boluch. "They told me to come back in three months, but I thought the war would be over by then so I immediately tried to find out where I could get on a ship. A couple of boys from town had attended King's Point Merchant Marine Academy in New York, and after a month they were on a ship, so I applied, and was accepted."

The grandson of freed serf slave farmers of the Polish Czarist Empire and the son of Ukrainian parents who in 1909 legally immigrated to what was then a Slavic farming community in Amherst, Massachusetts, Myron Boluch, a long time Scituate resident, is one of a rapidly diminishing group of veterans. Scituate American Legion Post Commander, Ed Covell, reports there are 147 WWII veterans in town.

Boluch attended Amherst grammar and high schools, graduating in 1940. When he wasn't going to school he worked on local area potato and onion farms.

Boluch enrolled at Amherst College on a tuition scholarship in the fall of 1940. He had just completed his first year and started his second year in the fall of 1941 when the Japanese bombed Pearl Harbor on December 7. Boluch would later return to Amherst and go on to Harvard Law School.

After a month's training at King's Point, Boluch found himself a midshipman in the Naval Reserve assigned to a cargo ship that was part of a convoy to England. There followed a series of assignments to cargo ships, and in early 1944 he was sworn in as an ensign in the U.S. Naval Reserves.

"On June 6, 1944, I was on an attack transport carrying 500 combat troops of the 29th Infantry Division to Normandy as part of the D-Day invasion force," he said. The 29th Division was legendary for being in the first wave at Normandy Beach, suffering massive casualties.

"These were all southern boys, and so many of them came from one town," Boluch recalls.

"The sky was gray with a low overcast; the sea was rough and it complicated the unloading of the men. I was up on deck overseeing the ship during the transfer of the assault troops to the landing craft. I had a clear view as the troops climbed down the netting hung over the side to the tossing landing craft. As each boat pulled away I watched; many never made it to the beach taking direct hits from the German shore batteries. We were just 250 yards off 'Easy Red' beach next to the cliffs of Point du Hoc. At night German bombers flew overhead. We had a near miss. All day and night it was constant roar. If you

Myron Buloch

looked back toward England, all you could see were ships. There was no time for sleep. There was never a quiet moment. Shrapnel from the shore batteries rained down on us; it killed some on deck and damaged the ship. This went on for three or four days as we continued unloading mobile guns and vehicles."

Upon return from England, Boluch was promoted to second officer assigned to the S.S. *Thomas Donaldson*, a cargo ship, as part of a convoy to take supplies—food, clothing, medicine, tanks—to the Russian Port of Murmansk. It was January 1945, as the convoy of twenty-six cargo ships and twenty-six escort vessels assembled off Scotland. "We headed up to the Arctic Circle above Murmansk where there were many German U-boats. We had heard that the German submarines were armed with the new acoustic torpedoes that could destroy a ship by just coming close. When we were about half way there we ran into a storm that lasted four days. The convoy was scattered all over the Arctic Circle."

It took time to regroup the convoy and Boluch recalled that the captain had been below to rest.

"We kept in touch with the other scattered ships by radio and signal lights to get in our assigned spot. Finally, I got between two ships so we would have some protection from the acoustic torpedo, but a British destroyer pulled along side and hailed us by bullhorn that we were out of position. Then blowing its 'whoop-whoop,' siren it pulled away. The captain came up to me on the wing of the bridge; he wanted to know what the commotion was. I told him everything is under control, but he didn't believe me. He spoke to a crewman; he stopped the ship dead in the water. When I disagreed with his order and said we should keep going as we were before he came on deck, I swore at him that he was going to kill us all. He ordered me below. As I sat down in my chair in the officers' mess, a huge explosion blew my chair and me up and bounced off the overhead. All went dark. I could feel the water coming in and I knew the ship was sinking. I relied on emergency fluorescent lights to make my way out to the port deck.

"Just two lifeboats remained and I was in one that held fifteen to twenty. It was freezing water and snowing; we lost sight of our ship as we moved blindly into the snow and ice. We got the boat headed into the wind. We could hear other ships. Four or five hours later a destroyer came by and signaled that they would not be able to stop, but that she would slow down and ordered that we grab the nets as she passed by. "

Following the rescue, Boluch and the other survivors were billeted on a British destroyer that had been torpedoed in the stern. Eventually he and the other survivors were put on a convoy headed back home. He would go on to serve out the war in convoys carrying cargo from America to England for the 8th Air Force bombers based there.

When the war ended Boluch was discharged and returned to Amherst College, graduating magna cum laude in 1947. Three years later, in 1950, he got his law degree from Harvard Law School. "One week I got my degree from Harvard Law School and the next week I got orders back to active duty with the Navy."

The Korean War was breaking out and Boluch knew he had to go. He served as an officer on large cargo ships and a troop transport during the war. He was discharged from the Navy as a lieutenant commander in 1953.

Boluch's wartime experience prepared him well to practice as a maritime lawyer with a large firm in Boston. "I worked on the *Andrea Dorea* collision with the *Stockholm* case." He retired from practice in 2000.

Boluch married the late Louise Ann Doyle in 1955 and has four daughters and eight grandchildren.

He received many commendations and awards including the D-Day invasion medal. On October 8, 1992 in a special ceremony honoring Liberty Ship seamen, Russian Ambassador Vladimir Lukin presented Boluch the Bronze Medal for his actions on the deadly Murmansk run.

A TIME FOR WAR

Our Tuskegee Airman

Eugene Jackson

"I JOINED THE U.S. ARMY AIR FORCE [AAF] ON October 29, 1942 at the age of nineteen," said Eugene Jackson, a native of Portland, Maine. "I didn't want to wait to be drafted, so prior to my enlistment I had tried to join the Royal Canadian Air Force [RCAF], but since America had already entered World War II, they weren't taking any more Americans. Then I tried to join the Merchant Marine and got turned down because I was near-sighted. After that I tried to join the U.S. Coast Guard, but at that time they were only taking Blacks as mess attendants and I refused that. Then the AAF was recruiting in Portland, Maine, where I enlisted."

On July 19, 1941, the AAF began a program in Alabama to train African Americans as military pilots. The program was conducted by the Division of Aeronautics of the Tuskegee Institute, near Tuskegee, Alabama—the famous school of learning founded by Booker T. Washington in 1881.

"I took my basic training at Tuskegee. Being a recruit at a segregated base, I never had a chance to go to town. Back then, the white soldiers and officers got on the buses first, and the African-Americans were relegated to the back of the bus. I just didn't have the patience to wait."

Eugene Jackson was a mechanic with the Tuskegee Airmen. This circa 1945 photograph of him at age 19 was taken in Ramittelli, Italy.

After basic training, Jackson was sent to an airbase at Lincoln, Nebraska, for aircraft engine mechanics training. "It was segregated as well and the African-Americans were put in separate barracks, mess halls, etc. It was cold too, and some of the southern boys had never seen snow before. We northerners would laugh seeing them wearing two or three pairs of trousers and a few shirts. There were no African-Americans in command. There was a fellow there with us, Herbert Julean, aka, 'the Black Angel.' He had been a colonel and pilot in Ethiopia as part of Haile Selassie's Army. The AAF would not give him an officer's rating." After spending the winter months in Lincoln,

Jackson was sent to Chanute Field in Illinois where he studied aircraft instruments. From there he went to Selfridge Field in Michigan where he was eventually assigned to the 332nd Fighter Group. "This was a transition period, and we worked on P-40s and P-39s [early World War II fighter planes]," he said.

"In January of 1944, we traveled on an old Liberty ship from Hampton Roads, Virginia, to Taranto, Italy." In the meantime many African-American pilots had completed training at Tuskegee and were commissioned as 2nd lieutenants. "We were sent on to Montecorvino and Naples and assigned to the 332nd AAF Fighter Group where we serviced the four squadrons that comprised the Group. It was there for the first time I saw violent death when a pilot tried to land his P-39 with the wheels up. Soon, all the older fighters [P-39s and P-40s] were replaced by the newer P-47 Thunderbolts and eventually the P-51 Mustangs. In June of 1944, we moved from the 12th Tactical AAF to the 15th Strategic AAF located in Ramitelli, Italy, on the Adriatic Coast. From our base, our planes attacked Germany, including Berlin, and some flew long-range escort duty for the bombers."

The planes of the 332nd were known as the "Red Tails," and they racked up an enviable record in shooting down enemy aircraft including the Messerschmitt 262, the world's first military jet fighter introduced late in the war by the Germans. According to Jackson, the 332nd lost sixty-six pilots and thirty more were captured by the Germans after bailing out. His Group was awarded a Presidential Unit Citation.

"I served under General B.O. Davis, who commanded the 332nd, and in servicing his plane I got to know him personally," Jackson said. "While serving in Italy, the Italian people were very friendly. I and five of my colleagues received a Papal Blessing from Pope Pius the XII. It was like a private audience with the Pope."

After the war, Jackson remained in the AAF Reserves. In 1948, President Truman ordered the Armed Services to be integrated. "I was recalled to active duty from 1950-51 where I served at Langley Field near Washington, D.C. While there, my greatest experience was meeting General James Doolittle. In 1951, I mustered out." While in the AAF Jackson rose to rank of staff sergeant.

"I met my future bride, Constance E. Cordice, in Boston in 1952, and we married in 1955. We both graduated from Boston University, she with a Ph.D., and me with a Bachelors. We were married for fifty years. My wife passed on March 31, 2006. We had no children."

But one memory still haunts him from his days in the service. While his group was getting ready to ship out for overseas duty, he and his fellow African-American Airmen experienced institutionalized racism first hand: "The Italian and German prisoners had the run of the base," he recalled, "a privilege that was denied us."

Jackson estimates that there might be as few as ninety or as many as 300 Tuskegee Airmen still living. He is the only one from Maine, and speaks proudly of his heritage as coming from the oldest African-American family in Maine, its involvement in the formation of the Abyssinian Church there, the third oldest in the country, and his great grandfather, George T. Rubey, the first African-American elected (in 1866) to the Texas Senate where he served two terms. Recently, Congress passed a resolution honoring the Tuskegee Airmen with the Congressional Medal.

Jackson is a resident of North Marshfield, and a life-time member of the Satuit Veterans of Foreign Wars Post.

Some Things
to Crow About

Gordon O'Brien

T HEY COME FROM BROCKTON, COHASSET, HANOVER,
Hingham, Hull, Marshfield, Norwell, Quincy and
Weymouth—a loose knit group of mostly retired
men. Every Wednesday morning they gather in Hull to
share breakfast at the Red Parrot at 8:30.

They treasure their independence and eschew charters,
by-laws, membership criteria, subcommittees, attendance
requirements, and the usual penumbra of formality. They
don't take minutes. They typify that granite-like strain of
Yankee independence, or to paraphrase Groucho Marx,
they wouldn't join a club that would have them for
members. Their one concession to formal organization is
a name. They call themselves the "Chanticleers" (French
for rooster). Their backgrounds are diverse—from
lobstermen to lawyers, fliers to physicians. But they all
share one thing—a story. This is one of those stories.

"Patton died in my bed," Gordon O'Brien, a retired
lawyer from Hull said, casually introducing this footnote
to history. A regular at the breakfasts, O'Brien had been

Gordon O'Brien posing with his medals case before being awarded the Legion D'Honor by the French Consulate in Boston.

invited to speak of his World War II experience. He told of how fate brought him and General George S. Patton together on two occasions during the war.

By June 1941, O'Brien had completed two years of college and one year of law school in Boston when he was drafted into the Army in March 1942, completing basic training at Fort Stewart, Georgia. He was accepted into Army Officer Candidate School at Camp Davis, North Carolina, where he trained for thirteen weeks prior to being commissioned a second lieutenant as an anti-aircraft officer. After seven months service in Panama that included infantry jungle warfare training, the Army sent him to the "jungles of France and Germany."

By the spring of 1944, O'Brien found himself in England assigned to an anti-aircraft group.

"We knew the invasion was coming," he said. "Every place we went wherever there was an overhang of a kind of tree or carport there would be a truck or a tank hidden."

After more training in Wales, O'Brien was ordered to South Hampton, where he was attached unassigned to the Fourth Infantry Division. It was not long after that when the order for the Normandy invasion came down.

"We boarded the landing craft at night. If you were lucky you got a bench in the LST [Landing Ship Transport], otherwise we stood up leaning against each other. It was dark and cold," Obrien said, recalling the long night ride in the flat-bottomed craft that crashed against the waves sending an icy spray over the sides onto the occupants.

"The ride took hours. Some of the GIs got sick. Nobody knew where in France we were going," O'Brien said.

Only later would he learn that his destination was Utah Beach. "Everyone was scared," he said "We knew it was not going to be a 'piece of cake.' But when you are young you know they can't hurt me."

O'Brien recalls the gray dawn breaking, pulling himself up, and getting a peek over the LST's side.

"All I could see were boats," he said. "There was the constant roar of artillery—some far some close. It was constant thunder twenty-four hours a day, for the next eleven months."

The landing craft began to slow.

"We were in the first wave," O'Brien said. "As the landing craft neared the beach someone yelled, 'Ready boys.' You could feel the bottom of the boat scraping the sand. You had to really stretch up to look out, but when the ramp went down we could see the beach. I was about in the middle and made my way following the man ahead of me. When I first hit the water I said to myself, 'This is cold!' The water was up to my armpits and I remember carrying my M-1 over my head. The first thing I saw when I got into the water was a string of machine gun bullets hitting the water as close as you are to me. Then I said to myself, 'These guys are shooting at me. I better get out of here.'"

As he made his way through the cold water, O'Brien recalls that by feel alone he finally found the trigger grip of the M-1 over his head, and as the water got shallower, lowering the weapon and pointing it toward the beach.

"The beach was littered with sand dunes and there was an opening between the dunes and we headed for that opening," he said. "Some guys were crawling over the sand dunes. There were metal rail track barriers sticking up from the sand, but we avoided them."

As he moved forward toward the opening between the dunes on Utah Beach, O'Brien recalls the intensity of the machine gun firing coming toward them.

"Men were dropping all around getting killed or wounded. As soon as I got between the two sand dunes, I flopped on my belly. The artillery was screaming overhead. At that point, we just kept moving. Beyond and ahead the sand rose higher," O'Brien, said.

Spotting a still-standing structure up ahead and off the beach, O'Brien and his men rushed toward it, seeking shelter from the hail of bullets.

"We just kept moving forward toward the building and ducked behind it," he said. "We formed up and moved forward. Our shooting was a blur to me. We just kept moving toward the shooting."

After establishing the beachhead, O'Brien recalls one uncomfortable aftermath of the landing.

"Our wool uniforms were wet for three days after the landing," he said.

As a liaison officer between Corps headquarters and the battalion, O'Brien's job was to get the orders to the battalions up and down the line. To accomplish that he was assigned a jeep and driver.

"Snipers were the biggest threat around Normandy once the beachhead had been established," O'Brien said. "The first time I was hit, my driver, Curley, and I were in the jeep when a bullet struck the front tip of my steel helmet. It hit in such a way that the round was deflected by the helmet and it went up inside the helmet, grazing my scalp, and exited the top of the helmet leaving a big hole."

O'Brien recalls suddenly seeing a lot of blood and putting a rag on top of his head and the helmet back on. He then pushed on to complete his mission.

A TIME FOR WAR

Prisoner-of-War

Paul R. Brown

"I SAT WAY UP FRONT IN THE PLEXIGLAS NOSE of the B-24 bomber. I was alone there. In front of me and below was a nose gunner in a bubble. I liked sitting there. On the nineteenth mission, on April 1st, 1944, we were shot down by flak over Alsace Lorraine. The plane was on fire. The nose gunner came out of the bubble. He was going to jump out. I pulled him back, and said, 'Johnny, you got to put your parachute on.'

"Everyone who went into the Army Air Corps expected to be a pilot," Paul R. Brown, long time resident of Scituate, said. Brown, who graduated from Newton High School in 1937, continued his education graduating from Boston University in 1941. He was captain of the BU hockey team and graduated with majors in business and teaching. Brown enlisted in the Army Air Corps in August 1942. He married Helen "Petie" FitzGerald, a friend from Newton, in November 1942 during his early training at Santa Ana, California.

"I joined the Air Corps because they paid more money— an extra $75 or $100 a month flight pay."

Paul Brown enjoys a day in London, posing in front of Number 10 Downing St., home to British Prime Minister Winston Churchill.

Brown trained as a bombardier/navigator for an advanced bomber, the B-29, which was not ready for operational service. He received a commission as a 2nd lieutenant. So impressed with Brown's skills as a navigator, his instructors selected him to fill in an urgent need for a navigator on a B-24. He joined the crew in Watertown, South Dakota, in 1942, and soon they were flying missions out of England.

"We flew out of Tibbenham, England," said Brown, who served with the 8th Air Force, 445th Bomb group. "We flew daylight bombing missions to Germany and France. We bombed a section in the corner of Northwest France called 'Particle A,' where the Germans had their buzz bomb pens. We also flew to Berlin, Nuremberg, and Frankfurt. We mostly flew to the Frankfurt area where the Germans had their factories to produce guns and planes.

Referring once again to getting shot down over France, he recalled, "I was supposed to jump out the front clam shell wheel nose door. Only half of the door was open, but I still wanted to go through it. I got stuck. I couldn't get out and I couldn't get in. I was stuck in a burning plane.

"I went straight to *God...Please God, help me, what should I do?* So he told me what to do. Stick your head down as far as you can between your knees and the slip stream will probably pull you out. It's something you don't forget. So He was right, the slip stream pulled me out. The next thing I remember I'm in a cloud. I couldn't see anything but cloud...I thought I was in heaven. I finally looked up to my parachute canopy and I see two thirds of it gone. Going down I floated over a town, a forest, a lake. I landed in a plowed field. There was someone working in the field a few hundred yards away. I yelled to him, and he yelled back, 'Get down—stay down.' I tried to hide my parachute in a ditch...but I wasn't very good at it. And shortly a German on a motorcycle came across the field and captured me. He took my survival kit. He took my flying boots. He took my BU ring."

After being captured the German offered to let the bootless flier ride on the motorcycle, but it was so uncomfortable that Brown asked to walk wearing only his uniform and his slipper liners for his flying boots.

"The German was so happy for me that he said, '*Pour vous, la guerre et finis* [For you, the war is over].' But I have to go to fight the Russians.'"

Of his crew of ten, all survived; however, the co-pilot's parachute had a delayed opening just before he hit the ground resulting in a broken leg, and he stayed with underground for the rest of the war. "The Germans rounded up the rest of the crew and they brought them to this central area where I was," said Brown.

"That night they put us into an underground bunker, no food, no latrine. We froze during the night." They were then transferred to a French prison, and from there they were put on trucks and trains destined to Stalag Luft One in Barth, Germany, on the Baltic Coast. "They put us in wooden barracks with bunk beds. We had to eat in our rooms what food we had, often limited to half a potato a day or a piece of cabbage a day. I lost about forty-one pounds. Eventually the Red Cross and Salvation Army supplied us with books, athletic equipment, like balls and bats. It was a compound surrounded by barbed wire, guard towers, and we had formations every night and morning where they would count us. If someone was missing they would send out the dogs. They captured anyone who escaped.

"The war ended and the Russians came through our area. They theoretically released us. They wanted us to walk thousands of miles to the Black Sea. Our colonel, the highest ranking POW, talked them into allowing us to be liberated by the Americans. We eventually were flown back to France.

The only survivors of the crew today aside from Brown are the co-pilot and one other crew member.

After the war Brown settled in Scituate, and had a career as an electrical manufacturers' representative. The Browns' have a grown son and a daughter.

And what about Johnny the nose gunner?

"For years later he would call me up to thank me for saving his life," said Brown.

A TIME FOR WAR

SECTION FOUR

THE KOREAN WAR

A TIME FOR WAR

The Art Lover at War

Ubaldo "Ubi" Di Benedetto

F EW WHO SUFFERED THE NAZI OCCUPATION of their homes would live to serve in the United States Army in another war and another continent a decade later. Of that number fewer would go on to get two Masters degrees and a doctorate, publish three books on comparative art and literature in Spanish, author eleven articles for academic journals on comparative art, including an article in Italian on Boston art and architecture, receive a Harvard Chair for thirty years of teaching, and publish a successful science fiction novel. But Ubaldo "Ubi" Di Benedetto of Cohasset accomplished all the above.

"The Germans marched in soon after Italy signed 'The Pact of Steel' with Hitler in September 22, 1939," Di Bendetto recalled. "They occupied my town. They occupied my home; and they set up the post office on the first floor. They stayed there until the end of the war when the British came to liberate the town."

The jackbooted invasion halted Di Benedetto's academic studies in his first year of high school.

Ubaldo "Ubi" Di Benedetto

"First we were traumatized because we did not know what happened to my father. My father was with the Royalist Army." The Royalists put up a fight with the Germans, but they were no match for the Wehrmacht and the survivors ended up in concentration camps. "I did not see my father until a year after the war."

Born in the town of L'Aquila, Italy, located at the bottom of the highest peak of the Apennines about a hundred and ten miles northeast of Rome, Di Benedetto spent his early years there completing primary school and part of his middle school.

"After the war, I was lucky to get a visa as an exchange student and I came to America. I was interested in foreign relations." At the age of twenty-one, Di Benedetto arrived in Boston, without much money and not having completed high school.

"First I went to Boston Latin High because I needed to finish high school and learn more English." Getting a student visa to continue his studies he enrolled at Northeastern University. "I studied English, American History, American Art, anything that had to do with America because I wanted to learn everything about America—what they ate."

While at Northeastern he worked as a bellhop at the Somerset Hotel in Back Bay. "I lived at the YMCA for four years from 1948 to 1952. It was good. The YMCA was on top of the School. I could hear the bells so I knew when to get up for class. I lived on tips from my work at the Somerset and the hotel gave me a good meal before I would start working, plus a small salary."

Di Benedetto graduated from Northeastern University with a degree in liberal arts. He married Delia Nesto, then a recent graduate from Emanuel College, and future long-time teacher at Cohasset Public Schools. "We had met at one of these parties that they held for foreign students, and she spoke Italian because she was studying it. We decided to marry. We married in August of 1952. I wanted to remain in America and the only way to do it was to volunteer for the Army." This was during the Korean War.

"In May 1953, I went to Fort Dix for Basic Training. After basic I was assigned to ballistic meteorology, the science that collects information on missiles and shells and studies the effects of weather on their trajectories. I wanted to be an interpreter, but when I went to classification and assignment they said, 'No, you are going to weather school.' But I said I don't know anything about weather. 'You will,' they said. 'Now we will have a weather man and a linguist at the same time.' I went to Ft. Bliss, Oklahoma to study for ten months."

Di Benedetto was assigned to the 82nd anti-aircraft brigade and to a mobile station. "Just south of Seoul, we manned a big weather station on the airbase and observed weather in the aircraft that we flew. We conducted studies in case of attack from the Russians, Chinese or North Koreans; we were testing if the ordnance will fire properly in all kinds of weather. It was during a combat practice exercise there, that my fire team partner fired a bazooka prematurely. Due to the blast I lost the hearing in my left ear. Later, I lost two toes to frost bite. I was convalescing for about a month in a field hospital and from there reassigned to a weather station on Stanton Island." He still takes pride in the fact that he was named "Best soldier of the month" for March 1955. After two years of active duty he was discharged honorably.

His scholarship and writing in comparative arts led him to a career in teaching, beginning at Holbrook High School, followed by Hull High School. Using the G.I. Bill benefits he earned two Masters degrees from Middlebury College, and a doctorate from the University of Madrid through Middlebury College. His first job as a professor was at Newton College of the Sacred Heart and from there to the Harvard Extension School with classes at the day school as well. At a special banquet at Harvard, Di Benedetto was awarded a chair for his twenty-nine years of teaching.

"A friend of mine suggested that I might be a good fiction writer. In 1980 we went to Centerville for a writers' conference. After a week there one of the instructors, Robert Taylor, who wrote book reviews for the *Boston Globe*, told me that if I were serious about writing books of fiction, that I would have a good opportunity to publish. So I started writing *Polar Day 9*. I wanted to use my experience as a ballistic meteorologist in creating a work of science fiction." When *Polar Day 9* was completed, his publisher surprised him by saying, "Your name is too complicated—we will find you a new name." Thus Ubaldo ("Ubi") Di Benedetto became Kyle Donnor.

"In the Army we used to go to seminars where we were exposed to ideas of warfare, and we studied how the weather could be changed. This has now become a theme for my science fiction," said Di Benedetto who is at work on his second novel and a book on the Renaissance painter Giotto.

Always appreciative that his military service was his path to U.S. citizenship, Di Benedetto declared, "Nothing makes me more proud than to march with the veterans in the Memorial Day parade in Cohasset. I still wear the uniform that I wore in the Army."

A TIME FOR WAR

110 Days and 18 Hours

Paul Welch

P AUL WELCH OF SCITUATE, WHILE STILL A STUDENT at
St. Colombkill High School in Brighton, decided he
wanted to join the U.S. Marines. He was only seventeen
at the time. "My father, John Welch, graduated from
Boston Latin School with Joe Kennedy, Sr., and he tied
for first place in academic honors with Kennedy. I knew
he would not allow me to join the Marines, at least until
I finished high school. But, since I was underage, I
needed his written consent. I forged his signature on my
enlistment papers, and I joined the Marines in Boston on
February 8, 1947."

Although Welch enlisted for active reserve status, the
Marines assigned him to an inactive group in the 25th
Regiment—New England's only Marine Reserve
unit. This allowed Welch to finish high school, and make
excuses to his father for the weekends he was away for
training. Little did Welch know when he joined, that
three years later he and his platoon mates would be
charging up the wrong side of a hill occupied by an
overwhelming enemy force in a land he didn't even
know existed at the time.

Paul Welch of Scituate (*right*), shown here in a U.S. Navy hospital in Japan, receives his Purple Heart from an admiral, for wounds suffered in Korea.

"When I graduated from St. Colombkill in 1949, I got a job at Western Electric Supply," Welch said. However, his career with Westinghouse was soon cut short. "In December 1950, I got a call from the Marines to report for active duty in Boston. That very night we were on our way to Parris Island for thirteen weeks of boot camp. I was trained as an infantryman—0311," he said stressing the Military Occupational Skill (MOS) designated for that job. After boot camp, and a short leave in Boston, Welch was ordered back to Parris Island, and from there his company boarded a troop train to the Marine base at Camp

Pendleton, California, where he underwent advanced infantry training. "We were there about ten weeks; then we sailed to Japan as part of a 'replacement draft.' From Japan we sailed to Pusan [South Korea] for assignment. We arrived there on June 6th 1951." According to Welch, his company was designated as an "Item Company" with the 3rd Battalion, 7th Marines. "We were put on a C-47 [cargo/personnel plane], to be flown north. When the pilot started the engines, both of them caught fire. The fire was quickly put out, but this happened three times before we actually took off, and once in the air, the plane was so overloaded we never got above 700 feet." Perhaps, the flight was an omen of things to come.

"We landed near the Hwopan Reservoir on a makeshift field," Welch recalled. "We could see hundreds of the enemy who were moving against about 100 Marines, when suddenly the enemy started retreating across a field toward the hills in the distance. Just then, some Corsairs [Navy/Marine fighter bombers] came in at about thirty feet off the ground, strafing and dropping napalm on the North Koreans." Welch said he and his men joined the other Marines and headed toward the hills in pursuit of the enemy. The long pursuit was hampered by days of heavy rainfall that slowed them down and forced them to cross streams that had risen to eight feet in depth. "Our first major battle came when we were near a forward aid station and found ourselves surrounded. There were thirteen men in the aid station when an enemy mortar made a direct hit and killed all inside. We could see waves of North Koreans advancing toward us in the distance. Again, we were saved by the Corsairs, but some were shot down too." The pursuit and counter attacks continued all the way through to September.

"On September 12, 1951, we were ordered to take Hill 680—part of the Kanmubong Ridge in North Korea. It was dawn; we were at the foot of the hill, and everything went wrong," said Welch. "Because a major made a mistake, he ordered our platoon leader, 2nd Lt., George Ramer, to lead us up the wrong side of the hill."

Welch paused momentarily and left the room to return with a photo album fat with, citations, letters, and pictures, especially pictures. He opened the book to an 8x10 glossy of a handsome young man in civilian clothes. "This is Lt. Ramer," Welch said looking with affection at the portrait. "He was the nicest guy in the world. He watched over everybody—'Did you write home? Did they write you back?'—he would ask us from time to time, as he made his rounds talking to each soldier." Welch looked up from the album to continue his story: "We were about half way up the hill when— and you won't believe this—I actually saw a mortar shell land and explode about forty feet away. I was suddenly flying in the air and landed about fifty feet down the hill. A friend of mine grabbed me by the collar and dragged me to safety."

For Welch, after 110 days and 18 hours, his war was over. But not so for the others. He learned later that Lt. Ramer had led five of his platoon mates to the top. But since it was the wrong side of the hill, they were about to be overrun by swarms of the advancing enemy. Lieutenant Ramer ordered the men back down to safety while he stayed to fight a rear guard action. Using his rifle, grenades, and finally fists, he held the North Koreans off long enough for his men to escape to safety before the onslaught. Shot in the leg and one arm, Ramer fought on until they overwhelmed him, shooting and bayoneting him to death. Lieutenant Ramer would be posthumously awarded the Congressional Medal of Honor. "Out of the original band of 220 men that went up the hill, by the end of that day only five could still fight," Welch said.

After a long hospitalization, Welch mustered out with many medals including the Purple Heart. He worked for Boston Edison for thirty-eight years. Today, he lives in Scituate with his black Labrador "Oscar."

A TIME FOR WAR

"Ernie, the Man of Many Talents"

Ernie Wessman

"IT WAS LIKE DUNKIRK. WE CAME ASHORE AT NIGHT in an LST near where the Marines were trapped by the North Koreans," Ernie Wessman said. "The Marines did not have any vehicles. I had been separated from my unit and assigned to take seventy-six, two-and-half-ton trucks on an LST to evacuate them. Although, I was only a corporal at the time, I found myself in charge of all the trucks. As we liberated the Marines, we fed them. My mother had taught me to cook, and I set up a kitchen tent to feed five hundred hungry Marines [retreating] to the LST."

Although often called upon to use his many talents, background, and training to serve in different and sometimes difficult capacities with dissimilar units, Wessman modestly says, "My military career could not have been better had I planned it myself."

Wessman comes from a family of seven children from Norwell where his father ran a small convenience store. He attended Norwell High School, but he was needed at his father's store and, as Wessman tells it, "My father took me out of school to help out, but later I went back to Weymouth Trade School where I studied printing."

According to Wessman, at that time potential employers were reluctant to offer a job to someone just out of school who might have to leave for military service, so he joined the Army Signal Corps to "learn central office technology, radios, and other telecommunications equipment." But when Wessman was sent to Fort Gordon, Georgia, the Army had other plans and he was assigned to a cooking school and "the kitchen as a cook for a period." Then, in that mysterious military manner, he was ordered to Fort Benning, Georgia, "where I was assigned to a combat support ordnance company."

While most soldiers are trained for one military occupational skill (MOS), and spend their military careers doing that specialty, Wessman was an exception. "When I went to high school, I took a business course and learned to type and the Army gave me another MOS as a personnel clerk." According to Wessman, this proved very useful for he was able to sometimes write his own orders and travel under them. "[Although I didn't plan it] I lived like an officer. Even in Korea, I had a tent to myself, a jeep, and a driver."

During a one month leave back home in Norwell, while helping his father, he met a young woman who brought fresh eggs to the store. Her name was Marilyn Tuttle; she would become his future bride, but his leave was cut short when the North Koreans invaded South Korea.

"Three weeks into my month long leave, in July of 1950, I received orders to report to Fort Benning,

Ernie Wessman

Georgia. My initial responsibility as personnel clerk was to cut orders sending men to Korea. But in August of that year, I got my orders assigning me to the 3rd Infantry Division—destination Korea."

Wessman's unit shipped out from the West Coast and arrived in Korea about three weeks later. The situation there was dire. As Wessman recalled, "The Army's 24th and 25th Regiments had been driven south by the North Koreans, so the Americans had their backs to the sea." Despite the need for new troops, "General MacArthur decided that our unit was not yet ready for this new kind of war, and he sent us to Japan to train South Korean troops for the fighting."

"After about three months, when the 24th and 25th Regiments were fighting their way back to the north, my unit was sent to Pusan to join those Regiments with the job of supplying ordnance."

During this operation, Wessman's unit marched across Korea from the east coast to the west coast, always no more than thirty miles from the front. "[The] only problem being that since it [the front] was moving all the time you were never quite sure where it was. During the summer of 1951, my company commander allowed me to use his jeep and assigned me a Republic of Korea Army (ROK) driver who we called 'Supply,' because he could scavenge anything; and, of course, he spoke the language.

"One day, 'Supply' and I were headed back to where we had been just the day before visiting some of my old pals from Signal School, when suddenly we were confronted by a patrol armed with submachine guns. Fortunately they were American infantry who told us to turn around. They reported North Korean Army troops had over-run the area not long after we had visited. I never saw any of my old Signal Corps pals again."

"Another time, moments after we started moving toward the front and just got on the highway, the whole area where we had been parked erupted from North Korean artillery. Again, we were just lucky," Wessman said.

He returned home to Norwell, and after four years of active duty separated from the service on February 17, 1952; he married Marilyn Tuttle on February 23rd. In 1955, he moved his family to Scituate. The Wessmans raised seven children—two sons and five daughters—and have been married fifty-four years.

Following his service, Wessman used his Signal Corps background to work in high-tech industries. He was one of eight people chosen by his employer to have his name engraved on a space probe that was launched to Mars.

Wessman served as the former Commander of Scituate's Veterans of Foreign Wars Post, and was active in Scituate's American Legion Post #144. As part of his service to veterans, he helped organize monthly visits to the Brockton VA hospital.

A TIME FOR WAR

Our Memorial
Day Chaplin

Eleanor Grossman

"I FELT I HAD TO REACH OUT. THIS WAS MY WAY OF GIVING back for the training I received in the military, which stressed confidence and self-assurance," Eleanor Grossman said, speaking of her role as Chaplain with the American Legion and her attendance each year in the Scituate Memorial Day services.

Her Memorial Day begins early with the boat ride to where the harbor waters meet the sea. There, accompanied by other veterans, and sometimes active-duty personnel, from a small rocking boat she lays a brightly flowered wreath in the dark waters; a tribute and memorial to the fallen. As part of the ceremony, the Scituate Veterans of Foreign Wars Post's Honor Guard fire a salute from the small craft bobbing in the waves. Chaplain Grossman reads a prayer that she has authored and edits over the years. Following that, she is off to the Common to read the Benediction as part of the commemoration services there.

"In 1950, I enlisted in the Marines," Grossman said. "At that time, a woman had to be twenty years old, and had

Eleanor Grossman

to have her parents written consent, and had to weigh at least one hundred and five pounds." When she first tried to enlist three months earlier, Grossman met the first two requirements, but failed the third. "I needed to gain five pounds, and it took me three months to do it."

Grossman grew up in Somerville where she enlisted. "We traveled by train to Parris Island, South Carolina. It was my first train ride. There were just thirty-eight women in my platoon." Following her training, she was sent to the Washington, D.C., area where she served her enlistment. After her service, she moved to Newton where her desire to "reach out and give something back" motivated her to join Newton's Women's American Legion Post 440 in 1955. While there, she worked in

Veterans' Services. "That opened doors for such service for the rest of my life. I was elected to the office of Post Chaplain. Since I was a little girl I have always had stage fright, and I had to overcome that to serve in this capacity. My Marine Corps training helped me."

On July 12, 1961, Grossman was named an Honorary Recruiter for the United States Marine Corps. In that office she wore a Marine Corps uniform and served in Boston in many capacities, interfacing with not only the enlistees, Marines, and veterans, but politicians as well, including President Kennedy's brother and [yet-to-be senator] Ted Kennedy, and the then-House Speaker John W. McCormack. She is pictured in her Marine uniform in the *Boston Globe* of March 15, 1962, shaking hands with John B. Crump, then ninety-three and one of the last—at that time—surviving veterans of the "Indian Wars." The picture is captioned, "He'll join the Marines." During this period, one of the memories that Grossman cherishes is responding to the wishes of the families involved and attending with the American Legion Color Guard the final services for over one hundred Veterans.

"When we moved to Scituate, I called the town's Veterans Agent and offered to be of service in any way I could. I was assigned to read the Benediction at the Common on Memorial Day; and sometime later, I met Brian Young, then Commander of the Scituate VFW Post, who asked me to lay the wreath as part of the early morning commemoration in the Harbor."

Grossman currently resides in Newton with her husband, but says she "wants to move back to Scituate." The youngest of her three daughters followed her example and joined the Marines, and is now a veteran. Her son has served in the U.S. Army active reserves for twenty-two years and has attained the rank of staff sergeant.

Though Grossman works on her prayer each year in preparation for Memorial Day, the themes of service and sacrifice, and the unsaid message that "freedom is not free," remain in her Benediction as a constant reminder to us all. Our Chaplain memorializes these themes in part by a quote from a portion of a letter that Abraham Lincoln is attributed to have written to a Mrs. Bixby on November 21, 1864, when it was brought to the President's attention that this woman had lost five sons in the Civil War. President Lincoln's letter, while brief, is too long for Grossman to incorporate in her prayer, but she captures its essence. Here is the full text:

Dear Madam,

I have been shown in the files of the War Department a statement of the Adjutant General of Massachusetts that you are the mother of five sons who have died gloriously on the field of battle.

I feel how weak and fruitless must be any word of mine which should attempt to beguile you from the grief of a loss so overwhelming. But I cannot refrain from tendering you the consolation that may be found in the thanks of the Republic they died to save.

I pray that our Heavenly Father may assuage the anguish of your bereavement, and leave you only the cherished memory of the loved and lost, and the solemn pride that must be yours to have laid so costly a sacrifice upon the altar of freedom.

Yours, very sincerely and respectfully,

A. Lincoln

I Trained to Fly with Ted Williams

Ray Sisk

"TED [WILLIAMS] GOT ME INTO THE MARINE CORPS. During the final stages of Navy flight training he came into the barracks from the flight line one day just before lunch. 'Hey, 'Bush,' that is what he called me. I don't know why, maybe he thought I was a bush pilot or a bush league ball player. 'There's a note on the bulletin board that the Marine Corps is looking for pilots out of our graduating class.' So I checked the notice out, and it sounded good."

Ray Sisk, long-time Scituate resident and retired Marine fighter pilot, was born in Arlington, MA, and attended grade school and high school in Medford, MA, graduating in 1939. He entered Boston College (BC) right out of high school as an accounting major in the second class of the college's Business School. "I was in the class of '43, but we were accelerated when the war broke out and graduated in January '43."

Keenly aware that he was likely to be drafted at any time into the Army, Sisk was looking for alternatives. "I saw an add in the paper that the Navy was looking for officers," he said, "and if you were in college you could stay there until you got your degree. So, I decided to look into that, and that is how I got to be in the Navy flight cadet program."

Three days after he received his diploma from BC, Sisk was on his way to training.

"They sent about twenty of us up to a small civilian-run airport outside of Keen, New Hampshire, where we began our flight training flying Piper Cubs."

Flying with instructors, Sisk recalled he soloed after about ten to fifteen hours. When they completed the month long training, Sisk and his fellow trainees were sent to a Navy program at the University of North Carolina at Chapel Hill for three months ground school where physical training was emphasized.

"You had to take three major subjects like soccer, baseball, softball, basketball," Sisk said. "I choose baseball as one of my subjects and that is where I met Ted Williams in April of 1943, and we became friends." Wikipedia fills in some details: "Williams also played on the baseball team in Chapel Hill, North Carolina, with his Red Sox teammate, Johnny Pesky, in pre-flight training. While on the baseball team, Williams was sent back to Fenway Park on July 13, 1943, to play on an All-Star team managed by Babe Ruth. Williams hit a 425-foot home run to help give the American League All-Stars a 9-8 win."

Each stage of training presented more challenges, more assessments by the instructors, and the ever-present threat

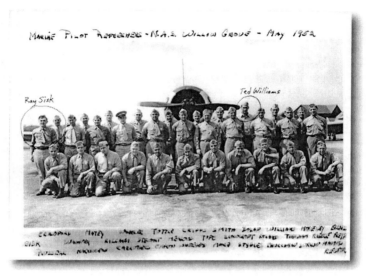

Ray Sisk (*far left, standing*), Ted Williams, and other members of the squadron reunited after being called up for duty for the Korean War.

of "washing out" based on those assessments. From Chapel Hill the trainees were sent to a small naval air station near Bunker Hill, Indiana. "Ted and I ended up in the same bunk room with ten other guys. We had a lot of ground school there. That was where we began studying navigation."

"Ted was at a big disadvantage," Sisk said. "He was one of the few guys in the group who was not a college graduate. He was dead set to get through the program. We worked out a plan. He used to meet with me after lights out. I gave him a short cut math course and he survived the tests. Once he did that, he knew he had it made. Johnny

Pesky [Williams' eventual team mate] was in the class too, but he washed out."

According to Sisk, flying open cockpit trainers in Indiana in late fall/early winter was cold. "We flew out of what was like a huge parking lot. You could land anywhere. Every once in a while someone would check you out in a two-seat version of the trainer, and they could wash you out and some did. I was lucky to make it."

The final training phase was Pensacola, Florida, where there were a number of outlying fields. "We were based at Sofely Field and later trained at Bronson Field, which was the last stop for naval aviators as they completed their flight training. "In my final check ride I flew with an instructor to one of the outlying fields. Once there, the instructor put the hood over me so I could not see out of the cockpit and he said now get us back home." The only way to do that, Sisk explained, was by flying on instruments alone. Sisk and Williams got their wings on May 2, 1944.

There was a necessary condition to become Marine Corps pilots. According to Sisk, "You had to volunteer. And Ted said let's put our names in. Two weeks later we got notices we were accepted and we took our commissions as lieutenants in the Marine Corps. Ted got his orders first. He was to be stationed in Pensacola. My orders were to one of the outlying fields south of Jacksonville. After welcoming us new pilots, they said, 'Now we will teach you how to fly like Marines.'"

The two men's paths would cross many times as they fulfilled their service obligations. Sisk would go on to ferrying much needed fighter planes from the East Coast to the West Coast and eventually end up as an F4-U Corsair pilot in Okinawa when the war ended.

After the war, Sisk retuned to BC Law School and became a lawyer. Williams returned to baseball and the two remained friends, with Williams giving him Red Sox tickets and calling him occasionally.

"I did not hear much from him until Korea broke out. It was at that time, in January of 1952, that I saw a headline 'Williams Recalled to Active Duty' and I thought if they got Teddy boy, it would not be long before they got me. The following Saturday morning my orders arrived to report. So Ted called me later in the year and asked, 'Hey, Bush, did they get you?' When I answered in the affirmative, he replied, 'The first western trip for the Sox I am going on [is coming up]; I want you to drive my car back.'"

Williams went on to fly Navy jet fighters in Korea, and Sisk, over his protests to get back into the squadron with Ted, was assigned to the Judge Advocate's office where, according to Sisk, "...there was an urgent need for lawyers."

Sisk was married to the former Mildred O'Keefe and they have two children, now adults. Sisk served ten years on the advisory committee in Scituate. He passed in 2014.

A TIME FOR WAR

The Forgotten War, Korea

Allerton "Al" Bonney

I T WAS JUST BEFORE THE DAWN HOURS OF JUNE 25, 1950, when Communist forces of North Korea attacked South Korea by crossing the 38th parallel. The surprise attack began with a thunderous artillery barrage to cover the 135,000 North Korean troops as they invaded South Korea. The North Koreans claimed officially that South Korean troops had crossed the 38th parallel. The North Korean forces were being advised and equipped by the Soviets, with tanks and other reserves. The surprise attack was a devastating success.

"On Monday, February 8, 1951, I was drafted into the U. S. Army," said Allerton "Al" Bonney, who was born in Scituate Hospital, no longer in existence.

Having mustered at Fort Devens, Bonney and the other draftees with him were sent by train to Birmingham, Alabama, and then by bus to Camp Rucker (Alabama) for Basic Training.

"I had the highest qualifying rifle scores in the Company during my twelve weeks of Basic training," Bonney said, "and was selected to go to Fort Benning,

Georgia, for fourteen weeks of infantry training and Leadership School."

Bonney returned to Camp Rucker where, he "... learned the fate of many of my buddies who had shipped out to Korea when I went to Fort Benning. It was not good news. In two years' time, forty thousand Americans were killed," Bonney noted.

After he returned to Camp Rucker, Bonney volunteered for the funeral detail which consisted of six men plus a sergeant. "To qualify for this detail you had to be at least six feet tall and handsome," Bonney said with a smile. [The funeral detail] was the honor guard the Army sent to escort the bodies of soldiers killed in action back to their homes. We escorted the casket to the services and then to the cemetery where we provided an honorary volley at the gravesite and presented the flag. I traveled to a dozen different funerals in Alabama and Georgia."

But the Army, in its wisdom, had other plans for Bonney. After a while it sent him to ordnance school at the Aberdeen Proving Grounds in Maryland for eight weeks where he trained in repairing everything from small arms up to weapons such as anti-tank guns, recoilless rifles and Quad 50s. "I was promoted to corporal in February, 1952," he said.

Meanwhile, dramatic events were developing in Korea. On January 4, 1951, Communist Chinese troops, which had earlier entered as allies with the North Korean forces, captured Seoul, the capital of South Korea. The U.S. 8th Army and the X Corps that occupied that area were forced to retreat. American morale fell. It rose when Lieutenant General Matthew Ridgeway, who had led airborne troops to victory in World War II, took over. By

Al Bonney in Korea.

March 1951, a revitalized Eighth Army attacked and drove the North Korean and Chinese troops from Seoul.

"When I went back to Camp Rucker after leaving Aberdeen, I found I had orders to go to Korea," Bonney said. Once in Korea, while standing in line waiting to take the train north to where the fighting was, Bonney was randomly chosen and sent to the Harbor Craft Transportation Corps, where, he said, "I was made the Company Armorer...and was in charge of the company's weapons and ammunition."

Aside from the job of armorer, occasionally he would "ride shotgun" on the forty-foot patrol boats that patrolled Pusan Harbor. At one point, the battleship *Missouri*, [upon which General MacArthur had formally accepted the Japanese surrender at the close of World War II] pulled in for re-supply. According to Bonney, the *Missouri* was sitting off shore shelling the enemy. For their actions in patrolling in Pusan Harbor, Bonney's entire company was awarded a Bronze Star.

By this time, Bonney's two-year enlistment was almost up, and, as he said, "My mother went into hysterics when she received a letter from my Company lieutenant praising my record and asking her to urge me to re-up. She was counting the days as I was."

Bonney gives much credit for his successful military career to another individual. "The man who had the biggest influence in my Army life was Phillip Brooks, a retired Navy officer, an expert sharpshooter, and a former member of the U.S. Olympic Rifle Team. He was the coach of the Rockland Rifle Team, which I had joined in 1948....Through the coaching I received from Mr. Brooks, I developed my natural skill in sharpshooting, which stood me in such good stead in the Army. My knowledge of guns and my ability at shooting made me a standout amongst the draftees who had never handled a gun previously."

As he reached his separation date, the war was coincidentally winding down. President-elect Dwight

Eisenhower fulfilled a campaign promise by traveling to Korea to find out what could be done to end the conflict. A few months after Bonney returned to the States to marry the girl he had met in Foxboro at a meeting of the South Shore Rifle and Pistol League before he went to Korea, a cease–fire was established on July 27, 1953, which set the front line at the 38th Parallel. A demilitarized zone was established around it. The DMZ is still guarded by North Korean troops on one side and South Korean and American troops on the other. No peace treaty has ever been signed.

Bonney has been married fifty-three years to Carmen "Dee" Bonney, originally from Lincoln, Maine. They have one son and two daughters, and six grandchildren ranging from age twelve to twenty-six.

A TIME FOR WAR

The Longest Winter

Lyle Thiefoldt

"I tHOUGHT I HAD IT MADE BECAUSE I HAD AN MOS (Military Occupational Skill) that would keep me in the rear," Lyle Thiefoldt said.

Born in the small farm community of Blaire, Nebraska, Thiefoldt attended high school in nearby Herman.

"When I got out of high school, I worked for my father who had a farm of about 240 acres of corn, soybeans, and livestock. When the Korean War came, I was twenty-one and got drafted. I had no deferment."

It was in March 1951 when Thiefoldt, fresh off the farm, reported for basic training at Ft. Leonard Wood, Missouri. "Basic training started out in cold weather then it got hot by May," he said. "It was an adjustment— taking orders from somebody. When I was in Basic Training I knew I was going to Korea. They were needing men badly."

Having completed Basic Training, Thiefoldt was sent to Fort Bliss, Texas, for antiaircraft gun training.

"It was a hot summer at Fort Bliss. We trained on Quad 50s and .90 mm antiaircraft guns. The course lasted about three months and I came home in September for a thirty-day leave." During this leave, Thiefoldt attended a dance and met his future wife, Mona. "I met Mona at a dance in North Bend when I was home on leave from basic training. Before I left the dance I got her name and address, and once I got to Korea I started writing her letters. She was writing back to me and to her brother Bill who was also there, but I did not know him."

After his leave, Thiefoldt was ordered to report to Fort Lewis, Washington, for debarkation to Korea.

"I was at Fort Lewis about a week and we shipped out. We went by troop ship and there were about 5,000 on the ship. This was in September 1951. We ran into a typhoon, and rode it out. I did not get seasick. Our first stop was Yokohama, Japan, where we got off the boat for processing and then got back on."

From Japan, the troop transport sailed to Inchon, Korea. "It took a day to two to get to Inchon. The troop ship could not sail into the harbor so LSTs were sent out to the ship. We climbed over the side, down the rope webbing that had been lowered to the LSTs. As we neared the shore, our LST's front plank was dropped and we ran for the shore."

It was September 1951; just five months after President Harry S. Truman relieved General of the Army Douglas MacArthur of his command for making public statements that contradicted the administration's policies. And it was almost exactly a year since MacArthur had conceived and

Lyle Thiefoldt

executed the daring amphibious assault at Inchon Harbor. However, the General followed up his victory with a full-scale invasion of North Korea on Truman's orders; China intervened in the war and inflicted a series of defeats, compelling MacArthur and the American troops to withdraw from North Korea. And so it was when Thiefoldt arrived at Inchon as part of the 5th Regimental Combat Team.

Once ashore at Inchon, it was time for assignments. "We formed up and we asked where the anti-aircraft gun was, and they said, 'We don't have any.' My MOS went down the drain. It was early October. There was a processing center tent a little ways down the beach and I went in there. I was unlucky. I was assigned to the Fifth Regimental Combat Team (RCT), which was infantry. They changed my MOS to 11B10 [Light Weapons Infantryman]. We were issued M-1s and combat gear, tents, and a bed roll (about forty pounds) to carry with us."

"From Inchon," Thiefoldt said, "they put us on a freight train. We did not move out until dark. The train took us to a destination west of Seoul close to the front lines."

When the Chinese entered the war, they chased the Allies out of North Korea and drove the line back to near Seoul. "We were going to be part of the push back," said Thiefoldt.

"It was not too cold and we were wearing cotton fatigues. I found out that the Fifth Regimental Combat Team was always attached to other divisions, and I found out we did their 'dirty work.' In that capacity, the 5th RCT's role was to be the spearhead—first up the mountain to the ridge, and there, to build bunkers for reconnaissance and firing positions for defense. If they encountered opposition, that would call in artillery. The plan was to leapfrog from hill to hill setting up recon bunkers, leaving Regimental Combat teams behind to do recon and run patrols and then on to the next hill, always pushing the Chinese back on the hills to the North beyond."

Once off the train at the base of the hills that rolled in like waves from North Korea, Thiefoldt realized they were practically at the front line. "I could see Seoul from a distance, but I never got there. Our job was to push the Chinese back. Our orders were to just take one hill after another and we kept moving toward the 38th Parallel. It was in late October or early November when we got there."

Once up on the top of the ridge, in the storied tradition of the American Army's prodigious reputation for digging defensible redoubts in record time since Bunker Hill, Thiefoldt and his men started digging.

"We built bunkers, and then we dug trenches all along the front line at the top of the ridge. We used our entrenching tools; the ground was rock and sand. There were places we could not dig deep enough so then we had to put up sandbags. We were looking down from the top of the ridge facing the hills of North Korea. There were trees on our hill. We had some of the South Korean people who worked for us, and we asked them to cut the trees down behind us and bring the trunks up to the top where we were, and used [them] to cover our bunkers lay[ing] sand bags on top of the trunks."

Once the lead element reached the 38th Parallel, headquarters ordered a halt to further progress. "We'd stay up on the line for a month and then they'd move us. At first, we're fighting North Koreans and then the Chinese. It was all mountains. We'd climb a hill and if there was too

Lyle Thiefoldt (*right*) and unidentified fellow soldier posing at the mouth of a bunker on a ridge somewhere in Korea.

much opposition we would back off. And then the next day we would try again. The RCT was the lead element and the others would follow. Once up on the ridge, we would stay put and the others would go ahead to another hill. "

It was tough, close fighting. "The Chinese used mortars and small arms against us," he explained, "and if too severe, we sometimes had to pull back. They had no airpower, while we did, and at that time we were moving them off the hills pretty good because we were cutting of their supply lines.

"From our firing positions on the top of the ridge we were e looking down the hill into North Korea. It was like that all up and down the ridges of the hills. These were defensive positions.

"We just stayed there and pretty near every other day we would pull patrols. We'd go north at night usually. We did a lot of night patrols. For a lot of them we had to go until we made contact. We had radios. I ended up being the radioman. The radio weighed thirty pounds. They always said the radioman was the first one they take out on a patrol.

"Sometimes we'd take a squad of fifteen or twenty on patrol and sometimes we'd take the whole company out. We would all be together in line, and seems like we were always on patrol. We would return to the bunkers on the ridge before daybreak. We had many encounters. Almost every time we went out, we lost guys to wounds and KIA. That's one thing—if anyone got killed or wounded we would bring them back.

"I was there from October 1951 to August 1952. We would go ninety days and they would move us off the ridge. And if headquarters had another hot spot they would send us there."

By then, the early tactical operations paid off for, as Thiefoldt explained it, "...Now wherever we went the bunkers were already built. The Chinese would be dug in on their hills and we would go against them. We had incoming everyday.

"It got cold and we were out in the field all the time. We would go in our bunkers. We had two-men bunkers. You could have no fire because any smoke would result in incoming rounds.

"It was snowing and freezing down to twenty degrees below. I never got frostbite.

"In the bunkers we'd pull guard at night. There were two of us in a bunker. We'd pull two-hour shifts, two on and two off. So when we were off, we just crawled into our sleeping bags and slept.

"We had little slot holes in our bunkers about a foot deep and put the weapons there, and I would be radioing headquarters routinely, and if we got into trouble we would call in artillery.

"We had air support and you could see them working on the supply lines—taking them out."

Throughout the long cold winter, Thiefoldt and his men stayed up on the ridge. As winter turned to spring, and spring to summer, there were rumors of peace talks.

Finally, talks over the armistice agreement started on July 10, 1951, in the city of Kaesong, a city occupied by North Korea in the North near the South Korean border. After a period of two weeks, on June 26, 1951, a five-part agenda was agreed upon; it would take another two years until the signing of the armistice on July 27, 1953.

"It was at this time, in July 1952, when all this was going on and they were having peace talks, when Headquarters decided that they wanted to straighten up the line, and there was one mountain out there that they wanted us to take.

"So the whole company went out on this one, as opposed to platoon or squad size. There were about fifty of us by then. So we took this mountain and got up to their trenches, and they started firing down on us. It was machine gun fire and this was at night. And all of a sudden they had us zeroed in and they started lobbing mortars. There was no cover. We had a Company machine gun squad. I had an assistant radioman with me that night. He was up ahead about 200 feet with the sergeant and I was in the back with the lieutenant. And my lieutenant got hit and I knew I had to maintain contact and so I went forward to the sergeant. When I got up there, my assistant radio operator had been wounded. And so then I took the radio to keep contact with the sergeant and the company commander.

"We decided we were losing so many guys that we retreated down the hill. The sergeant and I were the last men on the hill. We made sure that everyone got off.

"We were the last down the hill and when we were coming down we heard a noise, of course it was dark, and we hollered, 'Who's there?' And it happened to be this lieutenant and so I got him and carried him down to the bottom."

A couple of weeks after the action, Thiefoldt said that "They informed me that I was going to get an award. Another kid got the Bronze Star with a V at the same time. We went back to 5th RCT headquarters and the general presented us with the medals."

At the bottom of the hill, Thiefoldt and the squad leaders did a head count to ensure that all the men were present.

"The sergeant and I were the only two who were not wounded, and some of the men from the patrol were missing."

Once safely down the hill, the medic examined the

men. Noticing blood on Thiefoldt's fatigues, the medic directed him to the aid tent, where upon examination it was discovered he had a small wound to the abdomen. The medic dressed it and directed Thiefoldt to go to the field hospital for more treatment and processing. Thiefoldt asked how far that was and when he was told that it was a mile or so away he was so tired that he felt it was shorter and easier for him to return to his ridgeline outpost. Later, he would learn that had the wound been recorded his award would have been a Silver Star.

"We went back up on the line and continued the same routine. It was a point system and you got four points a month for being up on the hill. And if you got thirty points you were supposed to rotate home. But when I rotated home I think I had forty some points. But because we were losing people, and there were no replacements, and I was the radioman...

"So, finally, they gave me the good news. I walked down the hill to the company command post and that was where the cook was. And they loaded us on six-bys and kept moving us back to Inchon. From there, onto a troop ship to Yokohama, and then San Diego."

In total, Thiefoldt spent fourteen months up on the ridge.

Six months later, in June of 1953, Thiefoldt married Mona Jean. Thiefoldt went back to the farm in Nebraska where he had a successful career in farming, including planting experimental seeds developed at the university of Nebraska School of Agriculture that resulted in booster crops. He also served as a county commissioner. They have a daughter, Nicole, and a son, Eric, and three grandchildren.

SECTION FIVE

THE COLD WAR

Determined to Fly

Alan Labonte

"I WAS MOTIVATED. I WAS WILLING TO DO whatever was required. They needed two years of college; I got it. They needed my nose fixed. I was a very determined young man."

Alan Labonte of Scituate wanted to be a pilot. He chose the Marine Corps because, he said with a chuckle, "I liked the uniforms."

A 1959 graduate of South High School and former student at St. John's Preparatory School in Worcester, Labonte attended Worcester Junior College for two years studying engineering. He enlisted before graduation, but had to pass the demanding physical exam and have two years of college to enter the Marine Cadet, MARCAD, flight-training program.

"Every kind of exam you can imagine," Labonte said of this week of pre-acceptance physical exams. "They were pretty worried about my nose because I had a serious obstruction from playing football in high school. And so before I was accepted, I had to have surgery to open up the nasal passages."

Alan Labonte as a Marine Corps aviation cadet.

After passing all the exams, Labonte turned down an offer of entrance to the Naval Academy at Annapolis, Maryland.

"I think about that many times and say, 'I had my chance to go to Annapolis and I turned it down,'" he said. "I wanted to fly airplanes and in the shortest time."

The Navy runs the Marine Corps pilot training, and so, accordingly, Labonte reported for duty at the Naval Air Station, Pensacola, Florida.

"My first day in the Marine Corps was January 4, 1961," said Labonte. That's when he began the sixteen week preflight course—a combination of physical training, education and military training. "We were busy every day."

Everyone had to ride the Dempsey Dunker—a highly modified airplane cockpit located at the top of a high tower at the edge of a very large swimming pool. Once the trainee is strapped in, the instructor pushes a button and the device rolls down, slams into the water, tips over and then sinks to the bottom with the trainee, who must release the straps and swim to the surface.

"The first time I did it, my harness got stuck, and the Navy diver had to release me and shoot me to the surface," Labonte said. "I had to do it over again. As the instructor was strapping me in again at the top of the tower, I said, 'Look, I'm not sure I want to do this.' 'I'm sorry, sir, we don't have any time,' and wham—he hit the button and down I went. I said to myself, 'That's it. They're going to kill me. I'm going to drown, so I might as well just relax.' So the dunker went down. It rolled over and sank to the bottom and I just sat there, and said to myself, 'I guess I'm not going to drown after all.' I unstrapped myself and got out of the cockpit and kicked my way up to the surface, and I got a thumbs up."

At primary flight training, also at Pensacola, Labonte learned to fly the T-34, which was a tandem seat single-engine trainer.

"We (cadets) sat in the front seat; the instructor sat in the rear," he said. "Some of the instructors would just scream at you from the minute you got into the aircraft. I had a screamer one day, but most of my instructors were really good. I was lucky."

After soloing, the flight regimen became more demanding, "and that is where I started to run into trouble," Labonte said. "The instructors want you to consistently land in the first third of the runway. And that I could not do consistently. An instructor said to me, 'There's no question you are a good, safe pilot. If you were in the Air Force, you'd be all set, but in the Navy, you are not going to make it.'"

What Labonte did not know, and what all the Navy physical exams did not reveal at the time but what Labonte's neurologist surmised, was that he had contracted multiple sclerosis (MS) as a teenager. This no doubt affected his performance during the increased stress of practicing for aircraft carrier landings.

After "washing out," Labonte felt himself a failure, but still wanted to fly, so he spent a week in flight intermediate school located at another part of the base.

"There you go through a program of courses. After that an instructor asked me, 'What do you want to do?' I answered, 'Well, if I can't fly a plane, at least I could be in airplanes if I could be a navigator.' So they said fine, and they sent me up to Cherry Point, North Carolina in the spring of the next year."

According to Labonte, Aerial Navigator School was a very rigorous four-month course.

"That's where you learn how to use the stars, the sextant, and a lot of it is flying," he said. "We would fly in a four-engine plane outfitted with multiple glass domes. So trainees would go out as a group with our instructors and do our navigation, do star fixes and such. We trained at night mostly because we needed to see the starlight. You

Alan Labonte on Sandy Beach, Cohasset, MA (*photo courtesy Maryann T. Antonia-Loy*)

learn the stars; you learn the constellations, the names of the stars and then you learn to 'shoot the stars,' using the sextant to find your way in the long night flights."

Labonte graduated second in his class, receiving his navigator wings at Cherry Point where he was assigned to transport squadrons as an aerial navigator. Later, when the then new C-130s came in, "We started refueling jets. I was assigned to a mid-air refueling squadron. We could refuel three fighters at a time. It was tricky, especially at night. My job as a navigator was also to do the weight and balance, which is how the cargo and people are distributed in the back of an airplane, and to keep track of the fuel and weather. So I had a lot of work before we even took off. I would sit down in preflight and chart out the flight." This, he points out, was before computers were routine in airplanes.

"I always marvel to think that the light coming from millions of years ago, we were using to find our way," Labonte said. "In a religious way, if you are a good navigator, it would be hard to be a good atheist. It's humbling."

Labonte's service included being sent to Guantanamo Bay during the Cuban Missile Crisis in October 1962. He finished his hitch in July 1963, returned to Worcester and had a successful career. But his last career is another story best told by Labonte in his compelling book, *A Million Reasons: Why I Fought for the Rights of the Disabled.*

In 1990, Labonte was diagnosed with MS. Today, he is often invited to speak to companies, professional associations and groups regarding the rights of the disabled in the workplace. He lives in Scituate with his wife, Lora.

Labonte is on the faculty at Boston University, where he works at the medical campus engaged in health services research, working on ways to improve medical outcomes following surgery.

Chief of the Boat

Frank Moody

"THERE'S A PLACE UP THERE CALLED Okhotsk where the Russians have some of their main submarine and missile bases," Frank Moody of Cohasset said as he recalled, in a soft Kentucky accent, some of his real time "Hunt for Red October" moments as a crewman in 1959 on the diesel submarine USS *Spinax*.

It was another bright sunny day as the submerged submarine continued photographing Russian ship maneuvers while listening to their constant communications.

"That was when we heard the Russian sonar pings growing louder and closing in, alerting us to the start of a dangerous game of hide and seek. Several hours passed before we escaped the constant sonar pinging and threatening depth charges from the Russian destroyers. After assessing the damage, the captain made the decision to return to Yokosuka, Japan for repairs."

The story was never reported in any newspaper. Moody would become even closer to such threats of imminent destruction later in his career during several top secret underwater encounters.

A Paducah native, Moody joined the Navy in 1958, while studying engineering at the University of Kentucky. As the result of the Navy's extensive aptitude testing and evaluations, Moody was selected for submarine communications training, followed by one year of nuclear power training prior to reporting on board a submarine.

"While waiting for my class to convene for nuclear engineering school, I was assigned to the diesel submarine USS *Spinax*. During the tour of duty on the *Spinax*, we were deployed for six months with the Seventh Fleet in the western Pacific, which included a patrol off the coast of Russia," he said.

In 1960, Moody entered nuclear power school at Vallejo, California for six months of theory and then on to Pocatello, Idaho for six months of training on a nuclear reactor. From there he was assigned to the USS *Swordfish*, one of America's first fast attack nuclear submarines that operated out of Pearl Harbor.

"I was responsible for all the communications inside the submarine, everything from control to emergency communications systems. My tour on the *Swordfish* lasted from 1961 to 1963."

During one seven-month deployment with the Seventh Fleet, the *Swordfish* made two intelligence-gathering patrols.

"At some point on one of the intelligence gathering missions of a Russian military operation, we were detected," he said.

This incident was reported almost a quarter-century later in the *Chicago Tribune* of Monday, January 7, 1991:

The USS *Swordfish* submerged and was sneaking around a Soviet naval exercise in the Northwestern Pacific, an area the Soviets considered their backyard...a Soviet vessel had spotted light glinting off the *Swordfish's* periscope. The Swordfish dived for cover and a number of Soviet ships spent the better part of two days dropping depth charges here and there as they pursued it off the coast of the Kamchatka Peninsula in 1963.

According to Moody, the two-day cat-and-mouse game yielded valuable information through the *Swordfish's* extensive monitoring of the Soviets' capabilities.

"During the depth charge attacks they were close enough to shake the boat," he said.

A later assignment took Moody back to Pocatello as the senior instructor. "I taught the nuclear controls and electrical systems to qualify sailors on the nuclear sub," he said. "They had a prototype at the site in the middle of the Idaho desert that was the same as the ones on the nuclear subs. Admiral Hyman Rickover appeared in my class one day and stayed fifteen minutes. Later that day, the admiral requested my presence."

Aware of Rickover's reputation as the "Father of the nuclear Navy," and his penchant for critical and career ending interviews, Moody thought it was over as he stood at attention. "You did an excellent job. Keep it up; we need more like you," Rickover said.

After three years of teaching students in Idaho, Moody was assigned to the USS *Whale*.

Frank Moody showing off a prize catch.

"It was a state-state-of-the-art fast attack submarine designed for intelligence gathering," he said.

Following six months on the *Whale*, he was transferred to the USS *Darter* to address operational issues that plagued the sub during a training exercise."

After a successful cruise on the *Darter*, Moody was assigned to a series of specialty schools that included communications, surveillance and video systems, and was promoted to master chief (E9). At the completion of the extensive courses, he was assigned to the USS *Bancroft*, a missile submarine operating out of Rota, Spain, with a home base at Charleston, South Carolina.

Moody completed his qualification for the *Bancroft* and was selected as the chief of the boat (COB) reporting to the executive officer. As COB, he was responsible for the 115 enlisted crewmembers, their watch assignments and the material condition of the sub. The *Bancroft* carried sixteen fleet ballistic multiple re-entry vehicle missiles.

Moody spent his last tour at Great Lakes at the request of the commanding officer from the *Bancroft* who had preceded him there.

"My assignment was to address training and maintenance concerns with the gas turbine propulsion systems being designed for a new class of naval frigates," he said.

Working with the admirals responsible for the propulsion systems and the GE gas turbine division, Moody served in a critical liaison capacity, travelling between Great Lakes and Washington, D.C. His efforts resulted in modification of the frigates' monitoring systems, and an increase in crew training from five weeks to six months. For this three-year effort, Moody received the Navy Commendation Medal.

After his Navy career, Moody jointed ITT to work with six European divisions on improving software programming worldwide. From there, he went into sales and marketing corporate enterprise technology systems.

"As an avid fly fisherman and fly tier, I always found room on the sub to carry a fly rod with a fly tying kit to tie flies while underway," he said. "Stalking trout on small streams was my passion for forty-five years, but since moving to Cohasset, the pursuit of various salt water fish has replaced the trout. Also, since retirement, painting with water colors has developed into the same passion as my fly fishing."

Moody and his wife, Ann Jean, retired in 2003 and have made their home in Cohasset. They have four children and five grandchildren living in California, Colorado, New York and Hilton Head, South Carolina.

Congo Rescue

Marshall Litchfield

M ARSHALL LITCHFIELD TRACES HIS ANCESTRY back to Morris Litchfield, an early settler in Scituate in the 1600s. Born in Brockton, Massachusetts, Litchfield grew up in Braintree but was a frequent visitor to Scituate where he went to Sunday school as a child. He graduated from Braintree High School in 1951. Following graduation Litchfield attended the University of New Hampshire (UNH) where he majored in biology, played sports and joined the ROTC, partly to take advantage of some financial aid offered with the program. He rose to the rank of colonel of cadets, graduated and was commissioned as a second lieutenant in the Air Force in June 1955.

"After graduation we flew to Lackland Air Base in Texas for a month long orientation. That was the first time I had ever flown in an airplane." After successfully passing the orientation course and the rigorous flight physicals, Litchfield was sent to Marana, Arizona for primary flight training from October 1955 to April 1956.

Marshall Litchfield (*center*) and his crew of the C-130 Hercules.

"We flew T-34s and then T-28s. Both had reciprocating engines. I didn't like the T-28. It had a 4860 engine and it used to cough a lot. We did spin training; it had a terrible spin characteristic. When you tried to recover from the spin, it didn't feel the same each time. After a while you could tell who was going to be a fighter pilot and who was going to fly transports, and while I did well at aerobatics, flying fighters was not what I wanted to do."

From Lackland, those going into flying transports reported to Reese Air Force Base, Lubbock, Texas in May of 1956 for a six-month multi-engine basic training program. "We were flying B-25s (the same plane Jimmy Doolittle and his raiders used to launch an attack against the Japanese from the carrier U. S. S. *Hornet* in World War II. Flying the B-25s was a labor, they were old and decrepit, but I used to think about its glorious history and the kind of courage that would have taken to fly it off a carrier." At the end of this training period the pilots were given the opportunity to choose (from a list) their next assignment and base. "My father was not doing well. I chose and was selected for Otis Air Force Base on the Cape, so I could be nearby."

Arriving at Otis Air Force base in October 1956, Litchfield was assigned to the 962nd Airborne Early Warning and Control (AEW&C) squadron, part of the Air Defense Command 551st patrolling the east coast of the United States. The new assignment came with a new airplane, a C-121 Super Constellation, a four-engine, three-boomed tail distinguished by bulbous radar domes on the top and bottom of the fuselage designed to detect low flying aircraft seeking to penetrate U.S. air space along the east coast.

"No matter what the weather we had to go out; if there was a North Atlantic storm out there you would have to fly through it."

Litchfield became a pioneer pilot flying the then new and soon to be legendary C-130 Hercules. "The C-130 had an excess of power. It was faster and more maneuverable and adaptable, and it had great life-saving qualities for pilots. Our mission was taking care of all the U.S. forces personnel and bases in Europe. We worked with NATO and the UN. We had regular routes and 'You Call-We Haul' missions."

For the rest of his career Litchfield flew these missions. Some of them involved the highest security clearance and have passed into legend such as being one of two pilots selected to fly support for early U-2 spy flights over the Soviet Union. Yet his most fulfilling mission was to a place that few American Air Force pilots had been or would be in the future.

When the "winds of change" were sweeping Africa in the late 1950s and early 1960s the U.S. Air Force had a little known role in rescue missions, but the first and most impressive was during the Congo crisis. Like other nations in Africa, the then-colony of Belgian Congo was seeking independence from Belgium. A charismatic Congolese nationalist and Pan Africanist, Patrice Lumumba, had staged a coup on June 30, 1960 bringing down the government of the Belgian Congo. As the violence spread, the Europeans in the Congo were being attacked and massacred. The only hope for the Europeans was evacuation out of Leopoldville.

"I was there from July 8, 1960 to August 10, 1960. Our staging area was Tripoli." Litchfield and his crew did not understand the politics of this crisis, but came to understand how to mount complex rescue missions on a continental scale of over 3,000 miles in a hostile environment with warring entities. "Our job was to pick up military volunteer units from countries in Africa supporting the United Nations missions and transport them to crucial areas on the continent where they would 'keep the peace.'"

Litchfield recalls his first rescue mission: "Our destination was Leopoldville in the Belgian Congo. We took off from Tripoli and picked up troops in Morocco; from there we flew south over the Sahara desert stopping in Kano, Nigeria to refuel." But refueling, usually a simple procedure, was rendered impossible without enlisting the help of the local Sultan of the province.

"On approach to Leopoldville, I could see there were abandoned cars all over the airport but not on the runway, so I landed. It was a huge airport and we needed to get to the terminal fast to check in with the United Nations personnel. We knew the terminal was full of Europeans trying to get out. Our orders were to fly the injured from Leopoldville to Tripoli." But how to get to the terminal quickly became a challenge for Litchfield and his crew because of the distance from where they landed. Rising to the challenge the enterprising crew investigated the abandoned cars.

"The keys were still in the cars, so we commandeered an abandoned vehicle and headed for the terminal. When we got to the terminal, we entered from the back just in time to hear machine gun fire inside the building we had just entered. Someone was gunning people inside the terminal. It was chaos. We got out of there and headed back to the plane. When we got back to the airplane, local rescue personnel were scrambling to load stretchers with Catholic nuns. They were beat up, and some had been raped."

With the machine gun fire still rattling in the distance, Litchfield and his crew helped get every one on board and got the engines cranked and humming. They were airborne in record time. "So we got them back up to Tripoli for further evacuation to Europe. That was for me a sad mission. We made three more trips ferrying African security troops into Leopoldville, and wounded and injured out." To this day Litchfield considers that rescue mission one of the highlights of his twenty plus years of flying with the U.S. Air Force.

After completing his military service, Litchfield moved to Scituate. He taught science and coached four different sports at Thayer Academy for twenty-one years, retiring in 1992. Each year the Thayer Academy Hall of Fame Committee selects alumni who have achieved excellence in their athletic pursuits for induction into the Thayer Academy's Sports Hall Of Fame. Litchfield was inducted as a coach in 1998. He is a member of the First Trinitarian Congregational Church, and is on the board of the Scituate Historical Society.

Doomsday Sailor

Stephen Litchfield

O NLY UNTIL FAIRLY RECENTLY COULD the secrecy-shrouded story of Lieutenant Junior Grade Stephen S. Litchfield's naval service and the ship upon which he and his mates served be revealed. Litchfield 's service as a "Cold Warrior" was of such a highly classified nature that only certain individuals with the highest security clearances in the government, and who had a need to know, were even aware of the project. Ultimately he would serve on one of only two specially configured ships in the Navy. These ships were appropriately termed "ghost ships."

"I was born and raised in Scituate," Litchfield said. "On my father's side, I am a direct descendant of Lawrence Litchfield, who arrived just after the men of Kent (1636), and became one of the early settlers in Scituate. And on my mother's side, Nancy Wade Litchfield, I am a direct descendant of Nicholas Wade, who came to Scituate on the next boat after Lawrence Litchfield." Litchfield attended Scituate public schools.

Stephen Litchfield

"I was in the first class to graduate from the new high school in 1964. Our class claim to fame was that we were the first class to have four years at the new high school," he said. "I was a geek in high school, before the word geek was invented. I liked cars, mechanics, gadgets; electronics was my favorite. During high school I would fix televisions and radios for family, neighbors and friends. I did science fairs. My father had a garage, which had been my grandfather's, called "Ralph's Repair," where he repaired cars and other things. The townies called it 'Greenbush Tech,' because the guys who wanted to be mechanics trained there. My father taught everybody. I hung out there. My father was the best mechanic and machinist."

Following graduation, Litchfield was accepted at Rensselaer Polytechnic Institute (RPI) in electrical engineering. According to the institute's website, RPI "was established in 1824 as the first technological university in the English-speaking world..." While at RPI, Litchfield took the Navy Reserve Officer's Program.

"I was commissioned as an ensign two days before graduation in June 1968. I had not yet received orders, some of my classmates had already received orders to go to Vietnam, but then I received orders to the programming school at the Oceana Naval Air Station in Virginia. There were only five of us in that program. From there we got orders to a more advanced computer programming school for ten weeks in downtown Washington, D.C. Then I was assigned to my ship, the USS *Wright* (CC-2). It was a converted World War II straight deck carrier." According to Litchfield, the hangar bay of the ship just below the flight deck had been converted into a giant "War Room," a highly classified facility that required "top secret" security clearance for access. Inside was "the box," a state of the art computer system for its day, where Litchfield worked. On the converted carrier landing deck was a huge tropo scanner antenna that could not communicate beyond the curvature of the earth, which kept the ship always within 300 miles of the coast.

"Our mission was to provide command control and communications support in the case of a nuclear war.

Our job was to assess the post nuclear war damage and communicate our results....The ship was designed for the president to use as his command post in case of national emergency. The group we served with was called the National Emergency Command Post Afloat (NECPA).

According to a USS *Wright* webpage it was one of "two ships...uniquely configured and assigned the NECPA duties. The NECPA ships had to have good maneuverability to assure safe arrival, a reasonable probability of bomb effect avoidance, and were capable of state-of-the-art communications. The sister ships, USS *Northampton* and the USS *Wright* (CC-2), alternated the alert duty every two weeks as a potential floating White House/Pentagon. The NECPA strategy was to keep one of the ships somewhere off the East Coast. With only the customary naval acknowledgements, just outside of Norfolk, the ships would silently sail past each other as the alert ship was relieved in order to enter port for replenishing and much needed rest and recreation for the crew. The NECPA mission was a vital part of the Cold War for ten years. The men who served aboard the NECPA ships served their country well and contributed to keeping the world from a nuclear holocaust.

Litchfield spent a year and half at sea. With advances in satellite and submarine technology the two ships became obsolete. His ship was decommissioned in 1970. Litchfield was transferred back to Washington, D.C. for two more years working on computer systems. After four years of active duty, Litchfield left the Navy for a career in computer systems, including being the second systems programmer working for the City of Boston. "I married Martha Hines, who was my college sweetheart, right after I got into the Navy.

In December 2000 he returned to Scituate to the Wade family homestead. He is the immediate past Commander of Scituate's American Legion Post #144, and a member of the recently created Scituate Historical Commission. Interested in antiques of all natures.

"It was really interesting if you did not think about blowing up the world," Litchfield says of his Navy service as a "cold warrior."

SECTION SIX

THE VIETNAM WAR

A TIME FOR WAR

"Rising Above"

Robert Young

HOW DID A U.S. NAVY LIEUTENANT WHO "DROPPED OUT" following his final aerobatic flight test at the Naval Aviator Flight Training Center at Pensacola, Florida, end up earning two Air Medals over the skies of Vietnam? If you ask Navy Commander (Retired) Robert Young of Scituate he will tell you —it's his story.

Young, a long-time Scituate resident, was born in Hyannis, Massachusetts, and raised in Needham. "My brother was a career Marine, my father served as a Marine during World War II," Young said. "The family military history can be traced back to the Civil War and the War of 1812." As a child, Young was interested in the military, especially naval history, and he aspired to serve his country. Having graduated from Needham high school, he was accepted at the Massachusetts Maritime Academy.

"Life at Mass Maritime was almost the atmosphere of a reform school," he said. "There was just one building that served as a classroom, and no athletic facilities. No time off. The first year you were allowed

Robert Young

to go home for just one weekend a month. The food was terrible and we lived on an old ship. All three hundred cadets lived on a USN 1930s vintage auxiliary cruiser that would today be considered, size-wise, as a destroyer escort. We ate, slept, and showered on the ship. I lived in the engineer's compartment that housed about 120 men. We were packed in like sardines. The metal-framed, tied canvas bunks were stacked four high—basically cots. Even as an upper classman when it was lights out, I had two choices—sleep on my back or on my stomach, because [once in the cot], there was no room to turn over. It was a three-year program that ran year-round with only a Christmas break."

Just like Richard Henry Dana's 19th century classic coming of age tale, "Two Years Before the Mast," for Young serving as an ordinary seaman on a ship in a hostile ocean became a new way of life—a new challenge everyday. "We made cruises on the ship in the winter months. During our first year we did a cruise to the Caribbean and the next winter to the Mediterranean, and back again the third year to the Caribbean." Young graduated in 1957 receiving his Bachelor of Science degree in Marine Engineering, a license as a 3rd Assistant Engineer in the Merchant Marine, and a commission as an Ensign in the U.S. Naval reserve.

It was the height of the cold war between Russia and the United States when Young graduated. At that time many of the military's efforts, including those of the Navy, were dedicated to ensuring that there were no surprise intercontinental ballistic missile (ICBM) attacks on the U.S. from the Soviet Union. "My first ship was a Destroyer Escort Radar (DER) that was newly commissioned in Boston. We took it to Hawaii, our new homeport, and then made our cruises up and down between Midway Island and the Aleutians as part of a [sea-based] early warning radar system. The Air Force patrolled the top of the continental North America and the Navy monitored the Atlantic and Pacific Oceans. We were part of the Pacific Navy contingent of the Distance Early Warning Line [DEW Line]." Young served as a propulsion engineer on the ship for two years.

It was 1959 in Hawaii when Young met Eileen Doucet, an Army nurse at Tripler Army Hospital, and they were soon married.

When not on patrol, Young engaged in his favorite hobby—flying. "I was taking private flying lessons when the ship was in port in Hawaii," he said. After a while, he enjoyed flying so much he wondered, "Why should I have to pay for lessons when maybe the Navy will train me? So I applied to the Navy flight training school. I was a lieutenant, junior grade [JG] when I went to Pensacola. Classes were mixed with officers and flight cadets under the old Naval Air Cadet [NAVCAD] program. We flew out of Saufley field near Pensacola with an instructor. We flew the Beechcraft T-34, a low wing monoplane with tandem seating, with the instructor seated in the back seat." Young had completed six months of flight training when he was paired up with a new instructor for his last check flight. "I went up with a Marine major who I had never met for the final check flight. It was a turbulent day, " Young recalled with some still lingering anguish. "The turbulence was so bad that when the instructor told me to bank left, the plane bucked to the right. Frustrated, the instructor ordered me to land at a Marine airport that was new to me. I got a safety violation for entering the landing pattern at the wrong altitude. I was cut." To Young it was a devastating event early on in his Navy career.

As the new decade dawned in 1960, Young bounced back quickly with his new assignment to the cutting edge operational test and evaluation program at the Navy's Underwater Sound Laboratory at New London, Connecticut. "While I was there I rode evaluation missions on ships and submarines testing new equipment," Young said.

One of his most interesting projects was working

with the top secret, underwater sound and detection system, SOSUS, that was being built and tested (an ocean floor listening system to detect enemy submarines; think "The Hunt for Red October"). "I worked for Navy Captain Carl Sander, who was very inspirational and who motivated me to apply to go regular Navy," Young said, crediting Captain Sander for his decision to make a career out of the Navy. Young served at New London for three years.

"I then reported as a first lieutenant on board the USS *Wetstone*, a Landing Ship Dock [LSD], based in San Diego. "While on a West Pacific deployment, we were conducting amphibious landing exercises with the Marines in the Philippines when the Tonkin Gulf incident occurred in 1964. So we were ordered to the coast of Vietnam. We were the first ship to arrive off the coast of Danang. Soon, we were joined by fifty-three other ships."

In December 1964, Young, who had at one time volunteered to serve on "Swift" boats (small patrol boats), got orders to serve in-country. "When I arrived in Vietnam [on] January 1, 1965, there were about 22,000 Americans in-country." Young reported to U.S. Navy Headquarters in Saigon. From there he was assigned to serve with the South Vietnamese Navy as an advisor riding a variety of their ships and boats. One such assignment followed another. "I rode on all kinds of ships, jumping from ship to ship. As advisors we kind of created our own assignments. I volunteered to fly in the back seat of a single engine observation plane to spot targets and direct naval gunfire. Army pilots would pick me up in Piper cubs and I would provide the spotting, gun fire support, and coastal surveillance," he recalled. For that action, Young received two Air Medals. He then spent six months as an advisor aboard a thirty-eight foot wooden junk on coastal patrol.

Having finished his tour, Young went on to serve in many capacities for the balance of his twenty-four years with the Navy, including postgraduate school, earning a Bachelor of Arts degree in Middle East studies. He retired from the Navy in 1978 as a full commander, and then as a civilian had a successful career as a consultant to the Environmental Protection Agency, and continued to spend time at sea as a Licensed Master Mariner operating yachts and ferry boats along the Atlantic Seaboard.

Model Soldier

Gary Vitty

"THE LAST TIME I SAW MY MOTHER SHE SAID TO ME, 'You are going to go to Vietnam, and I will never see you again,'" long-time Scituate resident Gary Vitty said. His mother's prophecy proved uncannily correct, but not in the sense of her prediction; she died a week later. His mother's concern was justified in that, according to one source, the life expectancy of a U.S. Army second lieutenant Infantry officer in Vietnam was eight minutes.

In 1958, when Vitty, an only child, was seven years old, his family moved from Winchester, Massachusetts, to Stockbridge.

"My first job was for fifty cents a day, and it was for taking care of a dog," Vitty said.

The dog under Vitty's care was a unique dog, not in the sense that it was a rare breed with a long pedigree; on the contrary, it was a mutt that was rescued from the streets of Pittsfield. Its uniqueness came from its owner.

"The day we were moving in to our new home in Stockbridge, the man from next door stopped by. 'Hello,' he said, 'I'm your neighbor Norman Rockwell." Vitty recalls that neither he nor his parents recognized the man or his name.

Before long the Vitty's new neighbor offered the young boy the job of walking his dog, Pitter.

"Where did the name Pitter come from?" young Vitty wanted to know. The famous artist and illustrator explained that he had rescued the homeless and injured dog from the streets of Pittsfield, hence the name "Pitter." According to Vitty, Pitter loved to be in his master's studio watching quietly while the artist worked.

"Then one day, our new neighbor knocked on our door to tell us that he was going to Russia and asked if rather than putting Pitter in a kennel, I would take care of him. My parents agreed and I got to take care of Pitter while the artist went to Moscow to paint Khrushchev," Vitty said. "My salary was raised to one dollar a day.

"Norman had set up an account at the local store for Pitter so that I could get what the dog needed. When he returned from Russia to pick up Pitter, he asked me, 'Gary, how did Pitter like the Friskies, the Carnation Milk Bones, and the candy bars?'

"I knew I was found out," Vitty said, "but Mr. Rockwell was not upset with me."

It was during this period that the famous artist was commissioned to paint a picture commemorating the fiftieth anniversary of the Boy Scouts. "I was chosen to be the Cub Scout who appears in the picture," Vitty said.

Following the launch of Sputnik by the then Soviet Union, America began its come-from-behind race into space. After John Glenn, the third person and the first

(Left): Photo of Norman Rockwell, Gary Vitty *(standing)*, and "Pitter"—the dog that Vitty cared for while the famous artist was visiting the Soviet Union. *(Right)*: The poster Rockwell painted to commemorate the Boy Scout's 50th Anniversary, featuring Vitty posing as the Cub Scout *(lower right)*.

American rocketed into orbit, the country was in the grip of space fever. Norman Rockwell, the artist noted for capturing the spirit of America, painted a group of kids in a backyard trying to build a space capsule out of trash cans. "I appear in the picture as one of the kids," Vitty said.

"One day my mother invited Mr. Rockwell over for lunch after his second wife died. When we sat down to eat, Pitter decided to join us by putting his paws on the table. 'Just looking for tidbits,' Mr. Rockwell said. Later, the artist would commemorate this event in one of his famous pictures."

Not long after this event, Vitty was stricken with appendicitis, and was hospitalized. While there, he received an autographed photo of Norman Rockwell in his studio with Pitter and Vitty with the inscription: "1958 photo: Dear Gary, Pitter sends you his best wishes. He is lonesome for you. So are all of us. Sincerely, Norman Rockwell."

"I was fortunate to know Norman Rockwell: as my first boss, as an illustrator and artist, as one of his models, and as a neighbor. I never realized he was famous until one day he said to me with great modesty, 'If I had not had the God-given talent as an illustrator, I would have happily been a house painter.'"

Vitty entered Norwich University in the Fall of 1967. During his four years at Norwich, the oldest private military college in the United States, Vitty served four years in the Corps of Cadets and the Reserve Officer Training Corps. In May of 1971, he received a commission as a second lieutenant in the U.S. Army.

"During my junior year at Norwich, we were given a 'dream sheet' to select three branches in the Army, two of which had to be combat arms," said Vitty. "My first choice was the Adjutant General Corps, a non-combat unit; my second choice was air defense artillery; and my third choice was field artillery.

"In May of my senior year, the school posted a list of students and the branches of the Army where they were to be assigned. I had been selected for Infantry training," Vitty said.

"The following December, I traveled to Fort Benning, Georgia for a ninety-day intensive Infantry officer training course. At that time we all were pretty sure we were headed for Vietnam."

Toward the end of March 1972, just after graduation from Infantry school, surprisingly the powers-that-be released most of the graduates to reserve status. "We were told that the Army by this time had eight thousand infantry officers and we were not needed for Vietnam. We were released from active duty and returned home. In the following August, I was assigned to the 3/16 Army Infantry serving out of Brockton."

For the next thirty-one and one-half years, Vitty's service consisted of a combination of Army Reserve and National Guard Service. Vitty retired as an Infantry captain.

"I was ready to serve in Vietnam, but that was not to be. I enjoyed my time in the Army," Vitty said. He is a member of Scituate American Legion Post # 144. Thanks to Norman Rockwell, Vitty will be forever young in Scituate and will be remembered as a Boy Scout.

A TIME FOR WAR

Remembering the *Oriskany*

Jack Pyne

Y EARS LATER IN UPSTATE NEW YORK, after his war, after the fire, John "Jack" Pyne, accompanied by his wife, Polly, walked the site of an ancient battle field, where on August 6, 1777, eight hundred patriot militiamen walked into an ambush that resulted in the bloodiest battle of the American Revolution. Five hundred of the militiamen were killed or wounded, a sacrifice that helped turn the tide of the war opening the way for Washington's victory at Saratoga.

"I saw the place where General Herkimer was mortally wounded," Pyne said. But there was something else that Pyne wanted to see—something personal to him—the final resting place of an anchor from his ship named for the battle at this place fought so long ago: The anchor of the U.S.S. *Oriskany*.

"The two officers who took my cabin, which they wanted because it had a porthole, were killed in the fire," the long-time Scituate resident said. Pyne was recalling his service on the storied aircraft carrier, where he served as a staff communications officer for two deployments in the Pacific from July 1963 to July 1965.

This was a critical time in American history, spanning the prelude to and entry of America into the Vietnam War.

While a communications staff officer, Pyne was not always deskbound. "I made two arrested landings on the carrier, as a passenger, and I was helicoptered and lowered fifty feet to the deck of a moving destroyer," Pyne said. "Then, having completed the mission, hoisted back up to be lowered back onto the deck of the *Oriskany*. As the helicopter hovered over the pitching deck a helicopter crewman said, 'Don't worry, sir, I'll tap you on the back before we lower you.'" The tap never came and Pyne found himself suddenly dangling outside the chopper, being lowered.

Staff communications officer encompassed a myriad of duties, one of which was to escort guests and dignitaries visiting the ship. "I escorted Charmian Carr, who played Liesel, the oldest daughter of the Von Trapp family, in the movie the 'Sound of Music.' I also escorted astronauts and guests of the Secretary of the Navy," Pyne said.

"In my two years onboard there was only one call for battle stations. We received early warning that a Russian Bear Bomber was about two hundred miles out heading our way. As the Bear Bomber flew low over the ship closely escorted by our jets, I could see the bomber's tail gunner waving. The official report of the incident flashed to headquarters was, 'The pilots exchanged the international fighter pilots' salute.'

"Things started to get exciting when the Diem government of South Vietnam was overthrown in a coup. We were in Japan at the time." Orders came down

Jack Pyne (*center*) aboard the USS *Oriskany,* circa 1967.

for the ship to steam with all deliberate speed to the South China Sea off the coast of North Vietnam. It was from that place in the ocean, called "Yankee Station," that the ship began to launch bombing raids on North Vietnam.

According to Pyne, the grimmest day in the history of the ship was on October 26, 1966, after he had left. A fire started in a hangar bay killing forty-one men, many of them pilots.

Pyne observed that the *Oriskany* was the setting for two major movies: "The Bridges of Toko-Ri," and "Men of the Fighting Lady." In June 1963, just prior to Pyne's arrival, President John F. Kennedy visited the ship to witness operational readiness.

After mustering out as a full lieutenant, Pyne returned to Scituate in 1965 where he met his soon-to-be bride, Polly. He returned to graduate school to get his CPA, and he now practices in Hingham. The Pynes have two sons and two daughters, and fifteen grandchildren ranging in age from nineteen months to ten years. Former Commodore of the Scituate Yacht Club, Pyne serves as treasurer for "Road to Responsibility," serving disabled adults in southeastern Massachusetts.

The ship that had such a distinguished combat record in both the Korean and Vietnam conflicts was retired in peace in 1976. In 2006, it was cleaned, and on May 17th of that year scuttled off the coast of Florida where it serves on as a man-made reef.

"The Navy had a lot to teach, but it didn't take two years to learn, and the remaining time was worth it to be able to live in the United States," Pyne said of his service.

Winning the
Hearts and Minds

Roger Pompeo

NESTLED AMIDST THE BUILDINGS THAT COMPRISE the village of Cohasset are the offices of Roger Pompeo, M.D. There is nothing to suggest that the owner's practice was not always as a family doctor right out of a Norman Rockwell portrait, caring for his patients in town.

"Our hospital took care of all comers—civilians, military, Viet Cong," said Pompeo of his experiences in Vietnam during the war. "It didn't matter to us if they needed to be stitched up. We didn't care [who they were]. My experience was a lot different from yours and probably a lot of other people. It didn't matter what your politics were. [If you were sick or injured] I was going to try to fix you up and help you."

In his last year at Boston University Medical School, Pompeo was enrolled in the Navy's Senior Medical Student program. His commitment was to complete medical school and to go on active duty after internship.

Doctor Roger Pompeo (*center*) and two Navy hospital corpsmen waiting for their flight to Vietnam, 1967.

In early 1967, Pompeo was assigned to a group of twelve Navy corpsmen, three doctors, and an administrative officer. They trained together and were sent to Vietnam in September of that year as part of the Military Provincial Hospital Assistance Program (MILPHAP–N7), which was designed to "Win the hearts and minds of the people."

"My first friends in the group were Navy Corpsmen Leslie Carter and Gerald Sweeney," said Pompeo. "They were two enlisted men who were wonderful people." Prior to deployment, the team trained in Washington, D.C. for about six weeks. "We studied Vietnamese and learned a little bit about the culture."

Arriving in Saigon, the team flew by helicopter to the Kien Giang Province Hospital, located on the South China Sea coast near the capital City of Rach Gia. It was located in what was IV Corps, where Americans were not fighting the war, but acting as advisors to South Vietnamese forces. The team at the hospital had very little security.

"The war went on at night. Casualties would start to come in the next morning. And so we would triage; we had very little blood to give to anyone. We would operate first on the ones that could make it. We only had two operating rooms," Pompeo said.

In addition to serving the Vietnamese people in the hospital, Pompeo and his team made rounds. "We would make Med Caps. We would take these small Vietnamese boats out to the villages. The people knew we were coming. We would go to a village and have sick call. We had no security. Along the banks you could see young men of military age. I think they were Vietcong. I always felt that they were not going to hurt us because we were the only surgical capacity in the entire province. I didn't worry so much about getting killed, perhaps as I should have. I always felt that I would be captured and that they would put me to work doing surgery. I believe that our security was in knowing that we were there to help."

It was deadly dangerous work. If you go to the Vietnam Memorial Wall you will find Corpsman Carter's name on Panel 54, Line 27. Corpsman Sweeney was wounded in the same attack and subsequently succumbed. A third corpsman from the team, Richard Allen Nelson, stepped on a landmine and his name appears on the Wall on Panel 29 E, Line 97.

While Pompeo had done surgery as an intern and felt confident, the challenges in Vietnam were at a different level. "I look back now and I ask how did I do that? This one particular day there was a guy who was not going to make it so they assigned him to me, being the junior man. The guy was still alive so I took him in. He had a depressed fracture of the skull, so I took care of that. I closed a wound in his chest. I got down to his abdomen where I discovered a bullet had penetrated his liver and gallbladder. I had to suture the liver and remove the gallbladder. I had to do a colostomy and suture the small bowel. He was still alive. I was rolling him off the table and there was a wound in his back through his kidney, and I had to remove his kidney. I gave him two pints of blood. I said to myself, 'One patient and I did my whole surgical residency!'"

If winning the hearts and minds of the people was a challenge, winning the confidence of the Vietnamese physician colleagues was a greater one. "All Americans down in IV Corps were there to be advisors to their Vietnamese counterparts. But the Vietnamese doctors were too proud to have anyone give them advice. So what they did was to split the hospital into a medical obstetrics section and a surgical section. We ran the surgical section. Only one time in the whole year did they ask me for advice. A little pigmy lady was on her fourth pregnancy. The first three ended in miscarriages because her pelvis was so small that she could not deliver normally. This was her fourth and she was going into labor. And they asked me to do a C-section. They weren't trained for any surgery. So I did a C-section and delivered a little normal sized baby boy, and you should have seen the smile on her face. She was so happy; it was one of the most rewarding things I have ever done."

Pompeo vividly remembered another special patient, a young girl who had been seriously burned by napalm. "We operated on her several times. We had to keep her on intravenous feeding, but she was going downhill fast, and we were going to lose her in spite of the surgeries that were healing. Mercy Nichols, and some ladies from the Second Congregational Church in Cohasset, wanted to do something, wanted to make a contribution to the Vietnamese. So they talked to my wife, Ann, who suggested they 'send the money to Roger and he will do something.' This little girl was the first recipient. I took my interpreter, Co Cuc, downtown and we brought dresses, a little doll, food, and some toys. We went back to her bedside with all of these little gifts. People gathered around, including the nun who was nurse. I gave my little 'napalm girl' the doll. But she didn't know what the doll was for. This little girl had bandages all over her head and her hands. So we wrapped bandages on the doll the exact same way. She just lay there. She didn't know the concept of giving and receiving. And nothing happened. But the next day when we checked on her, she was outside playing with the other children."

Pompeo grew up in North Weymouth, moved to Cohasset for high school, where he played on the football team as an outside running back. "I married the quarterback's sister," Ann Chatterton of Cohasset. A Cohasset High School graduate, class of 1958, he attended Bowdoin College.

Pompeo has returned to his hospital in Vietnam for visits on two occasions, the second time with his wife about five years ago.

The Pompeos sponsored his interpreter , Co Cuc, who fled Vietnam after the war with the "boat people." They brought her to Cohasset, where she lived with them for a year. That is when she met her future husband, Nguyen, and moved to Jamaica Plain. Co Cuc named her daughter Ann, after Ann Pompeo. The Pompeos have four daughters and thirteen grandchildren.

There is a patient exam room in Pompeo's office where one might notice a small framed citation reading: "Bronze Star for Meritorious Achievement in ground operations against hostile forces, November 1968."

Love and War

Eli Mladenoff

"THE MOST INTERESTING INTERROGATION THAT I conducted [occurred] over several days…with a North Vietnamese Regular [army soldier] who had spent several years training in the Soviet Union. It was an interesting combination of Russian, Vietnamese, and English.…He offered a lot of good information on the Russian involvement in the training of Regular [North Vietnamese Army personnel] and insurgents [such as Viet Cong] in South Vietnam," said Eli Mladenoff of Scituate.

Mladenoff majored in Russian Studies and language while attending Youngstown State University near Youngstown, Ohio. He minored in Psychology and German. In his freshman year, he also joined the Army Reserve Officers Training program. He did an extra semester before graduating in January 1967, and was commissioned as a 2nd lieutenant. Shortly thereafter, he met Claudia, his future bride, on a blind date on her birthday, January 8. After completing basic Infantry training at Fort Benning, Georgia, Mladenoff was

Eli Mladenoff being awarded the Army Commendation Medal.

assigned to the Military Intelligence School at Fort Hollibird, near Baltimore, Maryland.

After completing the Army Intelligence School, with particular major and minors from college, Mladenoff thought he was assured that he would be sent to Germany. "I proposed to Claudia, and we were married on July 9th, 1967. But a couple of weeks before our wedding, I was advised my orders would not be to go to Germany, where I could take my new wife, but to Vietnam." With no time to think about the change in orders and the impact it would have on their marriage, the young lovers decided to go ahead and get married in spite of the almost immediate separation and unknowns of Mladenoff's pending assignment, which would put him in harm's way for a year.

"I left for the Republic of Vietnam one week after our wedding, and was assigned to the Combined Military Interrogation Center [CMIC] in Saigon, near Tan Son Nhut Airport." Mladenoff, who is proficient in learning languages quickly, also learned enough Vietnamese "to ensure accurate interpretation…With the exception of a few assignments to the Mekong Delta, I spent most of my time interrogating, writing reports, and counting the days until I could return to the 'real' world."

According to Mladenoff, he was known as an "easy" interrogator. "I never hurt a prisoner or even threatened a prisoner…I offered a comfortable alternative to the…cell, in a comfortable interrogation room with the prisoner sitting in a chair, allowing him to smoke and drink some cool water while [he was] telling me what I wanted to know."

Half way through his tour, Mladenoff got a week's Rest and Recreation, where he reunited with Claudia in Hawaii shortly after her birthday, and the first anniversary of their first meeting. "It was truly one of the most awesome weeks of my life, but going back to Nam after seven days of heaven was one of the most difficult things that I ever did."

It wasn't long after Mladenoff's return to Vietnam that the Tet Offensive began. "I was living at a Bachelor Officers Quarters [B.O.Q.] in Cholon, [the Chinese section of Saigon]. What we initially thought was a very loud celebration turned out to be an incursion into Saigon itself. The Viet Cong actually set up their headquarters at the Cholon PX, a huge department store for us military personnel, and just a couple of a blocks away from our B.O.Q. They didn't know we were essentially unarmed—

we only had a dozen or so hand weapons in the entire B.O.Q.—and [they] could have easily overrun us had they tried." Mladenoff admits he rarely writes letters, but said, "I used to write one or two a day to Claudia the whole year I was in-country. I would also do a voice tape every other day or so."

Like a lot of Vietnam veterans, Mladenoff faced scorn on his return. "On my return trip to the States, I flew by military transport from Saigon to Japan, and then to San Francisco. When I boarded the civilian flight [in Japan] to go to Cleveland and meet Claudia, the guy sitting next to me asked where I had been stationed. When I told him that I was returning from Vietnam, he turned his head and never said another word to me on the [long] flight." Mladenoff added that, "I have noted over the past ten years or so, however, that attitudes have changed [more positively] toward all veterans."

Among his Vietnam medals, Mladenoff was awarded the Army Commendation Medal.

The Mladenoff's raised four children—Nicole, Mandy, Josh, and Ali. All are now teachers, except Mandy, who is in public relations.

"The Best Traditions of Our Service"

Frank Giordano

"I HAD TO GO ON A MISSION IN A SINGLE ENGINE PLANE with a Turkish national. The weather was good when we took off from Ankara, but it gradually deteriorated into a blinding snow storm. Suddenly the pilot shouted, 'We are not going to make it!'"

If you go to "French Memories" in Cohasset around 8:00 a.m., you might see long-time Scituate resident Frank Giordano—though he blends in with the crowd— a habit formed from a long career as an agent with the Central Intelligence Agency (CIA). Spies can never speak of their professional successes, but they can share some unclassified anecdotes and public records about life in their service.

A native of Connecticut, Giordano graduated from Catawba College in Salisbury, North Carolina, in 1951, where he majored in sociology and business. He returned to his home state to work for AVCO Aircraft Company, located in Stratford, Connecticut.

"After about five years of working for the aircraft plant, I ran into a former classmate from high school who suggested I might try to get into one of the government agencies," Giordano said. "I spoke Italian and Spanish, so I submitted a letter to the CIA expressing interest in working for the Agency. I received a return letter informing me that they would have to do a background investigation. Six months later I received a letter setting up an interview at a nearby hotel."

At that initial meeting, Giordano took a series of written tests and when completed, his contact left with the promise that he would get back to him. He was back to work at AVCO for another six months when he received a letter inviting him to report to the CIA offices for more tests, including a polygraph at their headquarters which, at that time, was part of a four-building complex (HIJK) located on Constitution Avenue in Washington, D.C. A fully vetted Giordano began his career in the Agency in 1957, with his first assignment to the Middle East desk in Washington.

After a year and a half serving under the tutelage of a veteran officer, Giordano was assigned abroad to Aleppo, the second largest city in Syria.

"In 1959, I arrived in Syria. The U.S. Embassy was located in Damascus, and I was assigned to work out of the U.S. Consulate in Aleppo. Since I had no overseas experience, the chief of station worked with me. After a while, when the Chief traveled, I took over all the duties." According to Giordano, Syria was part of the United Arab Republic, UAR, dominated by Egypt, and not particularly friendly toward the United States.

Frank Giordano, far right, blends in with locals at a cocktail party.

"Sometimes I would receive anonymous harassment-warning calls late at night."

Completing his first two year overseas assignment, Giordano returned to Washington and to the then newly constructed CIA Headquarters, located in Langley, Virginia, where he was transferred to the Turkish desk.

In early November 1963, he was assigned to the U.S. Embassy in Ankara, Turkey, as a political officer. "I was walking up to my apartment in Ankara when I heard the news that President John F. Kennedy had been assassinated. Turkey and America were allies, and the Turkish citizens who knew I was an American expressed their condolences."

Giordano tells of a harrowing experience he had while flying over Turkey: "We crash landed near a remote U.S. airbase in eastern Turkey. We survived the hard landing but our damaged plane was suddenly attacked by a pack of huge hungry wolves coming down from the frozen mountains. 'Don't get out,' the pilot ordered. Then I heard shots. It was the Air Force guards shooting and scaring the wolves away so we could get out of the plane." In spite of the difficulties, Giordano and his colleague completed their mission. Giordano was by now fluent in Turkish and could pass as a native.

Completing his four year tour in Turkey, Giordano returned to Langley in 1967, to the Turkish desk. "But the Vietnam desk was taking officers from each and every other desk and they picked me to go to Vietnam."

In late 1967, Giordano arrived in Saigon and was assigned an apartment in a large building a few blocks from the U.S. Embassy.

"I got to know a Vietnamese woman artist who ran a nearby art shop. One morning she stopped me as I was going to work. 'Mr. Frank, Mr. Frank, can you help me?' she asked him. 'I have four children and tonight will be rocket attack. Can I bring my children up to your apartment tonight?'

"I brought them up, gave the kids ice cream, put them all to bed and I slept on the floor. And sure enough, a rocket attack occurred."

The 122 mm rocket that rocked Saigon in the pre-dawn hours of 31 January 1968 signaled for the sleeping city the coordinated communist forces attack against almost every important location and target in South Vietnam. A few blocks away from Giordano's apartment, Viet Cong (VC) guerilla suicide sappers had penetrated the walls and overrun the grounds of the previously invulnerable U.S. Embassy, killing a number of U.S. and South Vietnamese guards. The VC occupied the Embassy grounds for eight hours before they were driven out.

Once the Embassy was retaken, Giordano was there when a radio message came in from a besieged American unit fighting about ten miles away: "Rapidly running out of ammunition. Need resupply as enemy closing in." Giordano volunteered to provide the needed help.

"We hopped into a waiting truck and drove into the jungle to the ammo supply hut to load the ammunition onto a helicopter while under small arms enemy fire," he recalled. Not long afterwards the Embassy radio cracked again with thanks for the ammunition, which arrived just in time and resulted in saving fifteen American soldiers' lives.

For this action, Gordano received the CIA Citation of Merit which reads in part: "In recognition of his superior performance of duty while engaged in operations resulting from the Tet Offensive…in an atmosphere of widespread hazard, Mr. Giordano, working under conditions of great stress, demonstrated resourcefulness and high dedication in responding to the needs of the situation. The exercise of these qualities brought results of great value during a period of violence and confusion and adds luster to the best tradition of our service."

The Citation shares a place on the wall of the Giordano's home with an original painting presented to him by his Vietnamese friend whose family he helped save during Tet.

Just before his second tour in Vietnam, Giordano came to Scituate to marry Joan Grassey, a highly regarded secretary he met at the CIA. Joan's mother, Grace, was a long-time teacher in Scituate Public Schools. His new bride accompanied Giordano during his second tour in Vietnam. They have one son, Frank, Jr., and currently live in Scituate.

"Pole-Cat"

Dennis Badore

S TUDENTS OF SHAKESPEARE KNOW THAT THE TERM "Band of Brothers" comes from "Henry V." The play, which is of course fiction, is actually based on an historical event, the Battle of Agincourt (1415).

Like the Americans in Vietnam, the English troops were far away from home. The King had led his small English band across Northwestern France in an attempt to "win back holds in France that had once been in English possession." Outnumbered and with their escape route cut off, the English knights' morale was low as was that of the troops. It was time for leadership. King Henry knew he had to rally his troops, and he had to make the speech of his life. History records that the speech inspired his troops to victory. As Shakespeare fictionalized it some 250 years later:

> That he which hath no stomach to this fight,
> Let him depart; his passport shall be made,
> And crowns for convoy put into his purse;
> We would not die in that man's company
> That fears his fellowship to die with us…

We few, we happy few, we band of brothers.

There is no one that I feel this appellation applies to as appropriately as a member of that "band of brothers" than Dennis Badore of Scituate.

Let me tell you the story.

One day some time ago, I was in Tedeschi's in Scituate and I saw this guy with a Vietnam Veteran cap. Out of impulse I asked him, "When were you there?"

"'66 to '67," he replied.

"What unit?" I probed.

"First Signal Brigade," he answered.

"Wait a minute, that was my unit too. I was there '67 to '68," I told him.

Talk about a small world!

In his book entitled *Time-Line Vietnam*, Ray Bows devotes much of an entire chapter to Badore. He refers to him as the "Pole-Cat." As Bows writes, "I have met a lot of good men since my return [from Vietnam]....Among such men is Dennis Badore....Dennis's days in Vietnam in and around Long Binh were spent climbing poles, stringing wire for telephones and generators....There wasn't a better sniper's target in Vietnam than a signalman at the top of a thirty-five foot pole."

Bows recounts how Badore fell from a pole during his last month in Vietnam dropping thirty-five feet to the ground.

"I hit the ground with a thud," Badore said. "It took me a week and a half to recover from the impact, then I went back to work. Poles are just like horses, once you're thrown, you just have to climb back on."

Bows estimates that if all the poles Badore had

Vietnam veteran and Scituate resident Dennis "Pole-Cat" Badore stringing wire atop a pole near Long Binh, Vietnam.

climbed during his tour in Vietnam were stacked end to end he would have "attained a height of 120, 000 feet, or over twenty-two miles in the air."

A couple of years ago, my wife, Ethel, and I accompanied Dennis and Doris Crary Badore, who own and run the Oceanside Inn in Scituate, on a three day reunion of the Vietnam veterans of the 1st Signal Brigade. As part of the ceremony, the 1st Signal Brigade Association arranged to lay a wreath at the Tomb of the Unknown Soldier at Arlington National Cemetery in commemoration of the 237 service personnel from the 1st Signal Brigade whose names are inscribed upon the Vietnam Memorial Wall.

No one can witness the Old Guard's twenty-four hour, seven day a week Sentinel of the Tomb of the Unknown Soldier, with its majestic changing of the guard, without renewed reverence for this country and all those who have made the ultimate sacrifice.

To be present when a wreath is being laid before the Tomb in honor of the "band of brothers" with whom Dennis Badore and I served was a special moment that personalizes that sacrifice. It gave us the feeling that, as James B. Stewart wrote of another Vietnam veteran, Rick Riscorla, who died saving others during the evacuation of the Twin Towers on 9/11: "All the real heroes are dead."

Legacy of Vietnam

Ed Covell

S ECOND LIEUTENANT ED COVELL, SCITUATE resident
and graduate of Providence College, arrived in
Vietnam in early August 1967 to serve his year. He was
assigned to the 20th Brigade, 79th Group, 34th Engineer
Battalion located in Bien Hoa supporting the 173rd
Airborne Brigade.

"We were offered the opportunity by the 173rd
Airborne to send a squad of men to their jungle school,"
Covell said. "The week long program culminated in a
search and destroy mission where we went out into the
jungle to set up an ambush to interdict 'bad guys.' This
was for real. At around 2:00 a.m., two young Vietnamese
came walking down the path whistling, carrying lanterns,
a requirement for curfew. We thought very seriously of
going out and stopping them. One of the airborne
sergeants whispered, 'Let them go by.' We let them go
by." Hiding in the tall grass about 100 yards away,
Covell and his 150 trainees watched as nearly two
thousand North Vietnamese regulars followed down the

path. "It was probably the first true terror that I ever felt," Covell said." They never knew how close we were."

Back at base near Bien Hoa, Covell served as Headquarters Company Commander. He said that among his responsibilities was providing security for one fifth of the Bien Hoa Army Base perimeter, which was contiguous to the air base. He supplied personnel and equipment to the bunkers "which were the first line of defense." When he wasn't flying off to oversee his specialty detachments in the boonies, Covell spent his time overseeing the men and equipment in the bunkers.

Covell's men made time to help the locals. "Our battalion medics treated the Vietnamese children at a nearby Catholic orphanage," he explained. "During the Christmas truce of 1967 we treated all the orphans and nuns at the orphanage to a Christmas party where we gave them gifts." With the help of his sister, a flight attendant who took up collections for the orphanage, Covell's battalion supplied school uniforms to the orphans.

"We had intelligence about a week before Tet that a force of ten thousand Regulars and Viet Cong was descending on the Long Binh complex," he said. Covell "scrounged" up two quad-fifty caliber machine guns mounted on trucks and positioned them near his perimeter.

"Before the sunset of the night before the attack, a convoy of three-wheeled taxis came up Route 1 from the direction of Saigon into the city of Bien Hoa. There were three to six Regulars in uniform with their weapons in the taxis. We watched them go by. We had a no fire order

"A" Company, 34th Engineer Battalion, 79th Group, 20th Engineer Brigade, Commander 1st Lt. Edward F. Covell (*right*) and Company 1st Sergeant Clarence W. Futch stand at the entrance to the Battalion Tawk Bunker, Phu Loi, Vietnam, 1968.

that we respected." Before dawn on January 31st, the first day of the Vietnamese New Year known as "Tet," the attack on Bien Hoa began when sappers broke through the main gate at the air bases. "It was a war breaking out, no question," Covell said. "The Long Binh ammo dump explosion was notable and the shock wave was almost enough to knock a man over even at that distance."

According to Covell, it took three hours for the defensive air cover to get into the air. "They were Hueys at first, then gunships, then an hour later a flare ship flew over to light the landscape for the Spooky ships. When the Spookys fired, it was like the ground in front of us rose up two feet."

Throughout it all Covell and his men were still under a no fire order ostensibly to protect friendlies in the fire zone. The order came directly from Washington.

"On the sixth day after the attack things had calmed down enough for the engineers to do the cleanup. It was the kind of thing no man was ever meant to see....We buried 753 North Vietnamese."

After Tet, Covell was deployed to Phu Loi about twenty miles to the northwest where he became "A" Company Commander. From the time of Tet until his year was completed, Covell and his men were under constant attack. "A major responsibility was to clear twenty-five miles of road between Phu Loi and Cu Chi every day looking for newly laid mines," he said.

After his service, Covell worked as a chemist and later in management both in the United States and in England, and in France developing and marketing non-woven fabrics.

Covell returned to Scituate in 2003. A retired real estate agent for Jack Conway Company, he is married to Lorraine E. Weaver and they live in Scituate.

In addition to his Vietnam service medals, Covell was awarded two Bronze Stars. On July 14, 2008, he was installed as Commander of Scituate's American Legion Post #144.

The demons of America's longest war are tenacious and still haunt Covell as they do many Vietnam Veterans.

Jack P. Smith (b. 22 April 1945; d. 7 April 2004) opined on this phenomenon in a speech 8 November 2003, at the Ia Drang Survivors Banquet in Crystal City, Virginia, just six months before he died of Agent Orange complications:

> *We won every battle but the North Vietnamese in the end took Saigon....What on earth had we been doing there? Was all that pain and suffering worth it, or was it just a terrible waste? This is why Vietnam veterans often have so much trouble letting go, what sets them apart from veterans of other wars...I have discovered that wounds heal. That the friendship of old comrades breathes meaning into life...This has allowed me, on evenings like this, to step forward and take pride in the service I gave my country. But never to forget what was, and will always be, the worst day of my life. The day I escaped death in the tall grass...."*

A TIME FOR WAR

Strange Days Indeed

Bob Callahan

"I WENT INTO THE NAVY IN 1968 AMID AN upheaval of societal unrest over the Vietnam war. These were indeed strange times. Very confusing issues for an eighteen year old to deal with. It was a mix of changing sexual values, experimentation with drugs, and political unrest," said Bob Callahan of Scituate. For the young people today, that period probably has little meaning. But to Callahan it might just as well have been, as Charles Dickens said of the French Revolution, "It was the best of times, it was the worst of times...we had everything before us, we had nothing before us."

Callahan's observations on the year he made the existential decision to join the Navy are not without support. Author Mark Kurlansky wrote a book entitled *1968: The Year That Rocked The World.* In it, Kurlansky described the cognitive dissonance that affected all the young people of his generation who came of age at that moment in history, and the epochal events of that era, especially the overarching Vietnam War and the dark specter of the draft that, while only applying to men, forced

Radioman 3rd Class (RM3) Robert Callahan at the stern of the USS *Fulton*, a submarine tender, about 800 miles east of Washington, D.C., in the North Atlantic, 1970.

many, young men and women, into difficult decisions, life changing decisions. "At this time many young men tried everything to avoid being drafted," Kurlansky wrote. "We all knew somebody who was killed in action."

Taking his oath for the Navy was a proud moment, as Callahan observes: "There were a number of young men who decided they could not get a student or medical deferment, and so opted to head off to Canada to seek asylum. This prompted the First Navy District to take a group of new enlistees, of which I was one…to the USS *Constitution*, in Charlestown, to have us take the Oath of Allegiance on board 'Old Iron Sides'"

Amidst television coverage of young men burning their draft cards, some burning the American flag, Huey helicopters flying into battle in Vietnam, G.I.s wounded and in pain, Callahan opines of that period, "[T]he antiwar movement was one of the most divisive forces in twentieth-century U.S. history and it affected those of us who wore the uniform psychologically. Most of us were caught in the middle between the antiwar left, led by the Students for a Democratic Society, and the conservative right. Men and women wearing the uniform were thought of as bad…The antiwar movement became increasingly strident, greeting returning soldiers with jeers and taunts, spitting on troops in airports and on public streets. I too was spit at and called a 'baby killer' while walking through an east coast airport in uniform. . . . It became so bad that the Chief of Naval Operations authorized all sailors to be allowed to have civilian clothes [civvies] and to be able to leave their bases or ships in these clothes for their safety."

Callahan went on to serve with distinction on the USS *Fulton* (AS-11), a submarine tender, where, "[M]y job was to send and receive radio messages from our ship and the submarines in our squadron [Sub Squadron Ten] to shore stations," he explains. "[M]y ship was in the Atlantic fleet. I used International Morse code and radio teletype to communicate to shore and radio telephone to [communicate] with other ships and harbors we were entering. I was a petty officer third class radioman…

"I almost got washed overboard one night when a 100 foot wave [swamped] the ship while I was out on the bridge wing, but that's for another story," Callahan added as an afterthought.

In contrast to the reception that today's veterans are receiving upon coming home, Callahan noted, "When we Vietnam era service men and women came home we had no homecomings. We took our uniforms off and sneaked back into our communities to resume our lives."

An example of the recent resurgence in patriotism and respect for veterans is, according to Callahan, the reconstitution of the American Legion Scituate Post 144. Like so many other veterans of that era Callahan is finally beginning to feel the status of an honored veteran. "[Scituate American Legion Post] Commander [Conley Ford] asked me to carry the Navy flag in the Memorial Day parade [in Scituate] and in doing so I had my 'homecoming.' I finally felt like a veteran! I had given up years of my life for service to my country and now after watching people lining the streets applaud as we walked by I feel it was all worthwhile.

"This old sailor salutes all our veterans and especially those still serving, and please consider joining your local veteran group. The Scituate Post 144 welcomes all whether you served on the battlefield or in support of the battlefield, whether you served on a quiet ocean or a war torn ocean, it does not matter. All that matters is that you served your country when it was shedding its blood."

Ghost Soldiers

Paul Bucha

W ITH THE BACKDROP OF THE CAPITOL DOME, a pale moon white against the cold gray dawn and so close you could seemingly reach out and touch it, Paul Bucha was the final dignitary to address those gathered on November 10th, 2007, to listen to the speakers as a prelude to the march commemorating the 25th Anniversary of the dedication of the Vietnam War Memorial Wall in Washington, D.C. In the official program the parade was billed as "the 'welcome home' that many of our brother and sister veterans never had."

The prior speakers included Jan Scruggs, founder and president of the Vietnam Memorial Fund, and others who were instrumental in the long, arduous—and often thankless—battle for the right to erect a national memorial honoring those who served and sacrificed in Vietnam. Their dream came to fruition on November 13, 1982, when thousands of Veterans converged on Washington for the dedication of architectural student Maya Lin's stark black granite wall etched with the names of over 58,000 Americans who lost their lives or are still missing from America's longest war.

A TIME FOR WAR

More than fifty years since the last shots were fired and still the ghosts of Vietnam lingered, arching over all. As stated in the program: "Vietnam veterans were cast aside and forgotten by the country for which they had fought and died." The theme of the march was "Never again will one generation of veterans abandon another." And while the Wall was the result of the persistence of such groups as the Vietnam Veterans of America, it has become for the rest of the nation, a moving reminder of the price of freedom and the sacrifice of a generation.

A chilly wind heavy with drizzle picked up and the audience shivered under extra layers, as the still-handsome veteran mounted the podium. The murmurs from the group of Gold Star Mothers, Blue Star Mothers, Vietnam era military nurses, retired generals, other officers, enlisted men and on-lookers grew silent as they began to catch Bucha's closing remarks.

"There are the names of ten men on that Wall because of me," Bucha said pointing, as if symbolically in the opposite direction of the Capitol. "Those names are there because I made mistakes—because I didn't do my job. Had I done my job better those men would still be here now enjoying their families—their grandchildren." At that moment more than one handkerchief was discretely displayed as many teared-up.

"For conspicuous gallantry and intrepidity in action at the risk of his life above and beyond the call of duty, Captain Bucha distinguished himself while serving as commanding officer, Company D, on a reconnaissance-in-force mission against enemy forces near Phuoc Vinh… ."—so begins the citation that accompanies Bucha's Congressional Medal of Honor.

Veterans from around the country gather to march in commemoration of the 25th anniversary of the dedication of the Vietnam Memorial Wall in Washington, D.C., November 10, 2007.

"To paraphrase," Bucha continued, "the Medal of Honor Society doesn't encourage this, but I ask you, looking at the audience, do you see any members of congress, or senators up here on the podium this morning?" It was a rhetorical question. This was a bipartisan rebuke—for Republican Senator Chuck Hegel (R-NE) had been invited, and even Eleanor Holmes Norton, (D-District of Columbia-at-large delegate), a seemingly perennial presence at Washington marches and demonstrations, was absent. To be fair, Vietnam veteran Senator Hegel attended the ceremonies the next day at the Wall, as did Vietnam veteran, retired general and former Secretary of State Colin Powel.

A TIME FOR WAR

And soon it became time for the march to begin along Constitution Avenue to the final destination—the Wall. There were so many units in the order of march that it was scheduled to take place from 11:00 a.m., until 3:00 p.m. to allow time for all the units to pass in review. With some units, the wives, husbands, daughters and sons of veterans were invited to join their veteran spouse or parent, and in some cases grandparent.

To one who has had the privilege to march in the Scituate Memorial Day parade where enthusiastic crowds line the route, there seemed a paucity of spectators lining Constitution Avenue in Washington. Perhaps it was the weather, perhaps it was that it was a Saturday, perhaps it was that the march received little publicity, perhaps it was the specter that only those who were involved, or who had someone involved, really wanted to remember the Vietnam War. And so, ultimately, perhaps it was a march by Vietnam veterans for Vietnam veterans. One bright spot was the presence of our former South Vietnamese allies proudly in uniform lining the streets in spotty groups, enthusiastically stepping off the curb to shake the hands of their former allies. After the march my daughter asked me, "Dad, why would the Vietnamese be so supportive?" This question was a tribute to the efficacy of the anti-Vietnam War press and revisionist history that portrayed the American soldier as invading that benighted land—the Republic of South Vietnam.

"Because we went there to help them," I replied, "but then," I paused, "and in spite of our deserting them, they still appreciate the effort."

"Come Back, Come Back"

Doug Litchfield

W E MET IN DOUG LITCHFIELD'S FRONT OFFICE, sitting across from each other in folding chairs on a sun dappled driveway at his farm, Hillbilly Acres. It is a bucolic place filled with flowing water gardens, all varieties of plants and shrubs, rabbits, cats and seemingly all varieties of bird life. I heard a strange animal or bird call. "What is that," I asked? "It's a guinea hen," he said. His eyes were a piercing grey blue, he wore a panama hat and was dressed in gardening clothes, his hands were the hands of a man who works on machinery or plows.

"It sounded like, 'Come back, come back,'" I said to him.

"I was near Bridge #3, three miles from the Cambodian border not far from where the Ho Chi Minh Trail ended at the border between Cambodia and the Republic of South Vietnam, Litchfield said. "I was working on a self-propelled eight inch howitzer. It was appropriately named 'Delta Thirteen.' It was about 116 degrees outside, but down inside the machine it felt like about 160 degrees. I was trying to replace a generator and install a new one so the thing would work. I was alone; I was cursing the machine and the Army for still trying to operate such equipment. Suddenly, I hear this voice from outside. 'What's the matter soldier?' I was still cursing the machine, the heat and the Army as I emerged from its turret. The first thing I saw was the four stars, and then I read his name tag 'Westmoreland.' I thought I was in real trouble, but he just laughed and said, 'Calm down, you'll get it working.' We talked—he was just a regular guy. That's the way it was with 99% of the officers I met over there."

Litchfield, who is a life-long resident of Scituate, was in the first class to graduate from South Shore Vocational High School. He was drafted right around Halloween of 1967. After basic training at Fort Dix, New Jersey, he was sent to the Aberdeen Proving Ground in Maryland for advanced training on fuel and electrical systems for self-propelled howitzers and tanks. "I graduated with a perfect score and got a double promotion to an E-4 rank."

At the end of May 1968, Litchfield got orders for Vietnam, and was flown to Bhen Hoa Airbase and then onto Dak To, near the Cambodian border. "I was supposed to have six guys to support the work, but I was the only one." According to Litchfield he operated pretty much on his own out of Dak To. He was on call to service any vehicles that had broken down in the field in support of the Fourth Infantry Division. "A call would come in, and I would go up to headquarters tent, and get a ride on any chopper or plane that was headed for the area."

After his first year, he decided to extend his tour for another six months with a month's leave at home before going back. "I extended for two reasons. I thought they might let me out a little earlier, and because I had two

Doug Litchfield standing in a crater caused by incoming 122 mm rockets at the Dak To, Vietnam airstrip, June 1968.

brothers in the service—Steve was serving in the Navy in Washington, D.C. and Kenny was serving in the Army in Panama. I knew that under the Sullivan Act they could not send my siblings to Vietnam as long as I was there."

According to Litchfield, the first year was okay, and when he came home for the month's leave things seemed to be pretty normal to him. "My extension became a living hell. This was the worst six months of my life. No sooner had I returned then we heard President Lyndon Johnson saying on the radio he was halting the bombing of North Vietnam. We just could not believe it."

After that speech, it wasn't long, as reported by Litchfield, for the Ho Chi Minh Trail to become very active. "We were constantly under fire and in danger of being overrun by the North Vietnamese Army. One day, I had heard that we got some fresh chicken, and was looking forward to that, when suddenly we were attacked by 122 mm rockets. I dived for a bunker really trying to save the chicken from being ruined, and split open both of my thighs. They took me to the aid station and the doctor was writing me up for a Purple Heart, when I said, 'For what? Saving chicken?'"

His tour completed Litchfield, related going through Seattle Tacoma Airport to get a flight to Boston. "I was in my dress greens, and people were screaming when they saw me, 'Keep him away.' Just then a civilian approached me and handed me a first class ticket, and said, 'Get on the next plane and get out of here.' I never saw him again."

Litchfield said that during his extension America had completely changed. "When I came home, for a long time I was an emotional basket case. And there was no help, because no one knew about Post Traumatic Stress Disorder. Finally, I got some help; I go to the Veterans' Administration Hospital in Brockton." At one point in the interview he abruptly got up and returned with a twisted piece of metal and handed it to me. "This is the tail fin of the 122mm Rocket that killed my fellow soldier on guard duty."

Litchfield served honorably, and though he eschews medals and awards, still received many, including the Army Commendation Medal. He rose to the rank of sergeant. "I wasn't a hero; I just want to be a survivor."

Then I heard the guinea hen again, "Come back, come back."

Shot Down in Laos

John Andrew "Andy" Glutting

FORMER AIR FORCE INTELLIGENCE OFFICER Lt. Col. Al Shinkle has tracked American POWs in Laos for two decades. He says he has discovered that 324 of the 500 pilots shot down over Laos were still alive. He details a conversation he had with the Laotian Ambassador to Thailand in December 1985: "I asked him if they did indeed have American prisoners-of-war and he said, 'Yes, we have them in large numbers.' When I asked him if they were available for recovery, he said, 'Yes, they were for sale.'"

This is the true story of one pilot and his crew who were shot down in Laos, and lived to tell the tale.

It was August 1961 and the Air America H-34 helicopter that twenty-six-year-old John Andrew "Andy" Glutting was co-piloting lifted off from the Xieng Khouang Province air strip located in a clearing surrounded by the mist covered peaks and valleys of Laos.

It was his third week there and the former Navy flyer was copilot to an Army-trained pilot on an operational flight into Laos. "It was an orientation flight for me to learn where there were landing areas in the triple canopy rainforest," Glutting said. "Almost every day the cloud cover ceiling was low and it forced us to stay low—around three hundred feet—and we did not have any navigation aids (NAVAIDS) so flying was pretty much restricted to VFR (visual flight rules)."

After dodging in and out of cloud cover, one of the four passengers they were ferrying, U. S. Army Captain Karl J. Nagle, a Green Beret who had experience in the area, noticed that the terrain flashing by below should not have been there if they were on the route they were supposed to be.

"All of a sudden as we were flying, I heard this loud bang, bang, bang," Glutting recalled. A crewman checked for damage and reported the tail was riddled with holes. Oil was streaking back across the fuselage coating the doorway. "I told Dominick, the pilot, and we spotted a clearing and he brought it in for a rough landing." Glutting jumped out and ran head down and hunched shouldered to open the clamshell doors at the nose of the aircraft that housed the engine. "There was oil everywhere. I shouted up to the pilot, 'We're bleeding oil—they hit the oil cooler.' Dominick shouted back down to me, 'We got to get the hell out of here.' And I yelled back, 'We were not going to fly out.'"

With engine shut down, the only noise was the creaking and groaning of the bleeding chopper. As Glutting stood in the waist-high grass of the clearing, eyeing the tree line of rain forest just a hundred yards away, he reckoned the guerrilas who shot them down

HS-9 Helicopters operating from U.S.S. *Leyte* (CVS-32) during anti-submarine warfare operations. Note in foreground nose of AI-E Skyraider used extensively in Vietnam and fondly referred to by Navy and Air Force pilots as the "Spad" because it was designed in WWII. (Official photograph U.S. NAVY)

could not be far off. To complicate matters, he knew they were lost.

"The newspaper report said there were four of us, but really there were six—the pilot, me and the four passengers we were transporting into Laos," Glutting said. "We gathered around the wounded bird to figure out what to do. Fortunately one of the passengers was an Army trained guerilla, Captain Nagle. And he took lead of our little group."

The first priority was to come up with a plan of escape. "They gave us a training manual on how they

Andy Glutting competing in race at Marine
base Quantico, VA. Date unknown.

captured an American and kept him in a cage for a year,"
Glutting said, and he recalled the warnings from
intelligence briefings: the war in Laos is a secret war—
don't go down there. You are not supposed to be there.
"Our first instinct was to get away from the bird, out of
the clearing, and disappear into the dark shadows of the
triple canopy jungle carpeting the mountainous terrain a
hundred yards away. We grabbed the survival kit from
the chopper and ran to the temporary shelter of the tree
line and headed straight up the first mountain we could

find," Glutting said. Included in the survival kit was a small radio that would become invaluable in the coming days of escape and evasion.

"We used a bayonet to chop through thickets as we tried to put as many miles between ourselves and the copter," Nagle was later quoted in the *Boston Daily Record.* He was leading the group now and knew the area was controlled by a heavy presence of pro-Communist Pathet Lao rebels. The goal was to evade capture at any cost; they all knew the alternative was too grim to contemplate.

"I took a bearing to the north and we followed the compass in a straight line. We went up and down mountains and ravines. We forded streams. We cut our way through jungle so dark you could hardly see your hand in front of you," Nagle said. They had travelled a total of five miles by the time the daylight had surrendered to the night. They ended that first day and spent the first night on a coffee table sized ledge half way up a cliff in the spray of an icy waterfall.

At dawn after a sleepless night, the little band continued the escape and evasion. "We headed north because we figured that when we were shot down, we were south of Paquet, one of the CIA bases. A small plane flew over and we heard shots; the guerrilas were shooting at the plane. Now we knew both sides were looking for us," Glutting said.

"We had a small radio, but there was no food other than some dog biscuit-like rations. Toward the end of four days we heard a helicopter. Using the small radio we were able to establish communications. We set up a plan for a helicopter pickup. We radioed that we would be in a certain valley clearing on the map at a certain time.

As they neared the pickup zone they could hear the rescue helicopters approaching. "We could hear explosions getting closer to us. The crews of the rescue birds had not told us they would be dropping C-4 explosive charges as they neared the rescue site to make it sound like we had mortar support. But to us on the run in the jungle it sounded like mortars that were trying to zero in on us. When I heard the booms nearing us, I thought it was incoming."

The little band reached the pickup zone. "I could see two helicopters suddenly appear coming in and hovering low over the clearing without landing. I ran over reached and put my leg over the wheel and hung on. The others jumped onto the other two helicopters. They flew us back to Udorn."

When Glutting got back to Udorn he was reassigned to an airstrip outside of the capitol of Laos.

"It was just a landing field with three helicopters. One of the first or second missions I flew out of there was to aid some troops. Like before there was overcast but this time I was the pilot and I had just one crewman. We followed a narrow river valley. I did not know it at the time but one of the other helicopters had been shot at in that area the day before. All of a sudden I heard the familiar boom, boom, boom, and felt the bird shutter. The bullet went right through my seat wounding me in the leg slightly. So I was wondering how I was going to get out of there. I knew I had to get back down the river to return to my base, so that meant I would have to turn around and fly back over the place where I was shot at. I did not know what other damage had been done. Finally I just said f**k it; I just flew up into the overcast. I could fly instruments, but since we had no navigation radio signals I was half blind. Suddenly I broke out on top and spotted a nearby peak jutting out of the cloud cover. I landed in a clearing and a bunch of native people came out of the forest. Soon as it cleared up I checked out the bird and flew back to the base. I went directly to operations hut and handed them my resignation. I flew the helicopter back to Udorn and the next day I was on a commercial flight back home."

So how did a Navy pilot and admiral's son end up shot down in a secret war in a god-forsaken place where the chance of rescue was slim to none? Well, that is another story.

A TIME FOR WAR

"First to Communicate"*

Ronald Wheatley

"THE BRIGADE WAS THE FIRST TO ARRIVE IN Vietnam and the last to leave."

No, it wasn't Mel Gibson playing General Hal Moore in the movie *We Were Soldiers Once and Young*, it was Major General Susan S. Lawrence, Commanding General, Netcom/9th Signal Command addressing the banquet dinner at the biennial reunion of the 1st Signal Brigade on the occasion of the 150th Anniversary of the Signal Corps.

The 110 mostly Vietnam veteran attendees had served with the First Signal Brigade. General Lawrence was speaking at a Saturday banquet dinner of the four day reunion headquarters held at the Doubletree in Tucson, Arizona. It was fitting and proper that our former commander and group leader for the reunion, Lieutenant General Peter Kind (retired) made the closing remarks, for like General Hal Moore, he was always the first to arrive and the last to leave.

*Motto of the First Signal Brigade

The author next to his jeep at China Beach in Da Nang, Vietnam, shortly after surviving the Tet Offensive, 1968.

The program for Friday, September 17, the first full day of the reunion, was a trip to Fort Huachuca, the Army's super-secret mini National Security Agency (NSA); America's sentinel on the Western frontier just forty miles north of the US/Mexico border. The reunion agenda presented the opportunity for a first-hand unclassified look at how far the technology of the Signal Corps had advanced from our days in Vietnam when communications was line of site. This unobstructed line-of-site limitation required our signal posts in Vietnam to be located high up at the tops of places with names such as Black Virgin Mountain and Monkey Mountain, isolated outposts always vulnerable to being overrun.

I wanted to attend this reunion for many reasons, not the least of which was that it would be a trip back in time—for unlike many in the group, I had trained at Fort Huachuca. As the bus neared the Huachuca Mountains surrounding the fort, the memories began to flood in to that time so long ago when I trained there from early December 1966 to May 1967 immediately before being deployed to Vietnam.

"You men may have thought this was going to be a picnic. You're wrong this is going to be rough! You're gonna be cold and hungry and there will be times when you are gonna get mad. Never-the-less, you have some of the finest people in the Army training you and this will be a rewarding experience."

This to-the-point statement signaled the beginning of Exercise Dry Springs I. The speaker was a member of the tough, efficient Green Berets, who conducted the exercise to increase their proficiency in organizing guerilla operations.

It was January 1967 and he was addressing members of Ft. Huachuca's 160th Signal Group, participating in the twenty-four day field training exercise.

The morning was cold as we began the operation that involved 500 Ft. Huachucans and eighty Special Forces troopers.

"You," the Green Beret told us, "will be guerillas."

The words "no picnic" kept going through my mind as we loaded on to the waiting deuce and half trucks. We rode from base camp up into the hills that would be our home for the next twenty-four days. I couldn't help but smile when I jumped off the truck to find myself in the middle of a picnic area.

Green Beret "A" sergeant, aka Colonel Stienmetz (*far left*), inspects "guerrillas" before the mission.

"This is as far as the trucks go," someone shouted.

We had another formation and met our new section chief, a Special Forces sergeant wearing camouflaged tiger fatigues. He outlined the problem for us: We were now guerillas in the country of Arazan, which was friendly to the United States and which was being invaded by troops from a hostile nation to the north.

"I am no longer Sergeant Smith," our section chief said as he took from his pocket a camouflaged cap with a silver leaf on it.

"I am now Lt. Col. Steinmetz of the American Army, and I will be advising you along with the Special Forces 'A' team, which will arrive in a few days."

The author (*left*) and his wife, Ethel (*right*), with General Lawrence at First Signal Brigade union in honor of 150th anniversary of the U.S. Army Signal Corps.

at one point we "accidentally" looted a truck bringing us our own supplies. Like the first morning of the exercise the last one seemed especially chilly. We were dirty, hungry, tired, and cold. Just as we prepared to get into the trucks, I overheard another of the guerillas say, "Well, anyway, it started out like a picnic."

In May of 1967 we received our orders. Mine read to report to Oakland Army Base for deployment to Charlie Company, 37th Signal Battalion, 1st Signal Brigade, Chu Lai, (I Corps), the farthest northern U.S. military designated section of the then Republic of South Vietnam. I didn't know it at the time but I would get to the top of Monkey Mountain.

"Now the only thing you have to remember is that you are on bus Bravo. The bus in front of us is Alpha." The "counter-insurgents." We learned how to lay ambushes, how to practice field medicine and sanitation, how to move tactically, and how to live off the land. We went on night drops, recovery and re-supply missions. And finally we organized an all-volunteer "hatchet squad" for jobs requiring particular skills.

We got good at laying ambushes and were so hungry at one point we "accidentally" looted a truck bringing us our own supplies. Like the first morning of the exercise the last one seemed especially chilly. We were dirty, hungry, tired, and cold. Just as we prepared to get into the trucks, I overheard another of the guerillas say, "Well, anyway, it started out like a picnic."

In May of 1967 we received our orders. Mine read to report to Oakland Army Base for deployment to Charlie Company, 37th Signal Battalion, 1st Signal Brigade, Chu Lai, (I Corps), the farthest northern U.S. military designated section of the then Republic of South Vietnam. I didn't know it at the time but I would get to the top of Monkey Mountain.

"Now the only thing you have to remember is that you are on bus Bravo. The bus in front of us is Alpha." The announcement shook me from my reverie and I flashed forward to see General Peter Kind holding a microphone making the announcement up next to the driver, "So be sure you make the tour of the fort on this bus."

I knew I was really in trouble with the general when my wife, Ethel, and I left the first briefing of the morning a little late and ran for the second of the two buses and boarding it just as the lead bus, Bravo, was departing. "But, General," I said, "Bravo bus was supposed to be in back."

FIRST GULF WAR, IRAQ & AFGHANISTAN

A TIME FOR WAR

Scout

Forrest G. Teel

"MY TEAM WAS FLYING COMBAT SEARCH AND RESCUE. If an aircraft went down we would secure the pilot and either destroy the aircraft and leave, or secure the aircraft and wait for it to be taken out...I was sitting in the jump seat in the helicopter and I heard the order to change missions. I had five seconds to change the mission. We diverted to the new mission and captured the first POW's for the 82d Airborne Division during Operation Desert Storm," said retired Sergeant First Class Forrest G. Teel of Cohasset.

A 1975 graduate of high school, Teel joined the National Guard. "I wanted to be a police officer. While I was in basic training at Fort Knox, Kentucky, I thought I liked the life. I saw an in-service recruiter and I joined the regular Army."

Originally assigned the clerk typist military occupational skill (MOS), Teel soon found himself training to be a cavalry scout for the armored cavalry. "We trained in Armored Personnel Carriers (APCs). There was a lot of weapons training involved— everything

Sergeant. Forrest Teel (*center*) as a scout in Iraq during Operation Desert Storm.

the first POW's for the 82d Airborne Division during Operation Desert Storm," said retired Sergeant First Class Forrest G. Teel of Cohasset.

A 1975 graduate of high school, Teel joined the National Guard. "I wanted to be a police officer. While I was in basic training at Fort Knox, Kentucky, I thought I liked the life. I saw an in-service recruiter and I joined the regular Army."

Originally assigned the clerk typist military occupational skill (MOS), Teel soon found himself training to be a cavalry scout for the armored cavalry. "We trained in Armored Personnel Carriers (APCs). There was a lot of weapons training involved— everything into West Germany. "So if they just broke through the border there they could get like a hundred kilometers instant jump."

Teel summarized the Cold War exercises in Germany by saying, "It was always us watching them and them watching us. We always had no notice alerts with 3:00 a.m. calls. The scouts had ninety minutes to move out and occupy." Teel and his men spent a lot of time camping in the woods, living in tents, in the rain and snow.

"That's where I got to cross train with NATO forces," he said. "I trained with the Belgians, the French, the Italians, and the elite British Special Air Services (SAS) at that school and was picked to train at the Scottish Non Commission Officers Academy."

When he returned to the United States it was time to put his NCO skills to a test. "I applied to drill sergeant's school. I was accepted to train at Fort Knox, Kentucky." Of that experience Teel recalled, "There was a tough professional standard...It was like being on all the time." Teel graduated with honors and was assigned to a new unit, the 6th cavalry, for twelve more weeks training scouts.

"It was 24/7 and twelve to sixteen hours a day. So one of us would be the early man and one would be the late man. The early man came at 4:30 a.m. and left at 8:00 p.m.; the late man came at chow, around 8:00 a.m., and left at lights out."

"Where's my drill sergeant?" That's how every day of training at the Army's three-week intensive Jump School began for Teel. It was the early morning call of the jump school cadre's drill sergeant. He had a special place in his heart for former drill sergeant Teel.

"They had a thing called the 'gig pit,'" said Teel. "[It] was a big pit full of sawdust that was kept wet. They inspected you each morning. I'd pass inspection, but every day I went to the gig pit anyway. You had to crawl into the gig pit on your belly using your elbows and legs to push, but not up on the knees. Once in the gig pit they made you do physical training. And then you joined the others for the rest of the day's training."

Teel had risen to platoon leader, but there was still more specialized training. "We had to get the skills to be scouts for the 82nd, which required infantry tactics, airmobile tactics, among other things." Teel called this segment of his training the most physically demanding of his life.

"The thing I'd like you to know is that those kids were the best soldiers, bar none, that I ever had the privileged to serve with."

On August 2, 1990 the Iraqi Republican Guard invaded Kuwait and seized control of that country. That triggered a United States response, Operation Desert Shield, to deter any invasion of Kuwait's oil rich neighbor, Saudi Arabia. On August 7, deployment of U.S. forces began as Operation Desert Storm.

"We got the word to go; we were a follow on force for the 24th mechanized division. By then we had our Humvees and so we performed recon for the division. Because the 24th mechanized was in front of us, it was a swath of destruction as we followed. We were ahead of the 82nd since we were its scouts. We went all the way to just south of the Euphrates. We wound up at a place to turn around, near Talleial Air Base in Iraq. We secured the airfield and we took hundreds of POWs out of there." A hundred hours after the war began, President Bush declared a cease fire.

Teel completed his twenty years of service and retired. He went on to earn both a bachelors and a master's degrees in Computer Science. He works for General Dynamics as a systems engineer in Taunton. Among his many military decorations is an Air Medal.

A TIME FOR WAR

Night Flight

Rick English

"WHEN SADDAM HUSSEIN INVADED KUWAIT on August 2, 1990, we were one of the first aircraft carriers to actually leave the east coast to go over to the Red Sea," Rick English, a fifth grade science teacher at Jenkins School, said.

English attended Villanova on a Navy ROTC scholarship and was commissioned in 1986 upon graduation. He earned his wings as a naval flight officer in 1988, and was assigned to Carrier Airborne Early Warning Squadron 125 on the USS *Saratoga*.

Born and raised in New Kensington, Pennsylvania, he went to Valley High School where he was active in sports, running track, and in the Boy Scouts. After graduating from high school in June 1982, in September of that year he entered Villanova University, near Philadelphia, where he majored in political science. Having an interest in serving in the military from an early age, and with two older brothers who had preceded him in the military, he chose the NROTC at Villanova over applying to the Naval Academy as a way to serve in the military and have a way to help pay for his education. As part of the program, each summer the cadets "go on a cruise," usually serving on a ship or on a military base. After the second summer cruise, where he had the opportunity to fly in different aircraft, English decided to opt for the Navy Flight Officer (NFO) program.

English graduated and was commissioned an ensign in May 1986. From there he was sent to Pensacola, Florida, for initial flight school. The year long program began with ground school where trainees studied engine mechanics, navigation, aerodynamics and weather. After this initial trimester, those who were going to be pilots branched off to pilot training, soloing and getting more stick time. "Those of us training to be naval flight officers had to concentrate on navigation, weather, and communication with other aircraft that were up."

This primary flight training part of the process involves a series of real time exercises with five to eight flights in different aircraft practicing essential skills for the mission. For example, in English's case, training began with Navy's entry-level trainer, a single-engine prop plane, the T-34, with side-by-side seats; he transitioned to the more sophisticated tandem seated P-2 jet with pilot up front, and the NFO trainee in the back. This part of the program was a flight segment.

"Sometimes it would be a long flight and sometimes less so. The pilot gives you the score sheet on how well you did your fuel management, navigation, and communications." Transitioning to the Lear Jet platform provided the luxury of a corporate jet with new challenges.

Following this segment of training the candidates were

given a choice of one of four aircraft: an A-6 bomber, an EA6B Prowler as a controller; an F-14 as a radar intercept officer; an S-3 anti-submarine; and the E-2 Hawkeye. I was selected to train to fly in the E-2 Hawkeye, which is an all-weather, carrier-based twin turbo prop aircraft with a twenty-four-foot radar dome on the top." The aircraft's mission is airborne early warning and command and control aircraft.

"The E-2 Hawkeye is a five seat configuration with two pilots up front in the cockpit and three NFOs in the back. It is not a large aircraft so the three NFO's workspace is cramped with few creature comforts. The back of the E-2 was very small—an arm's span wide from the radar screen to window.

"Sitting shoulder to shoulder, in the far back is a small head. You have to walk bent over along a twelve-foot passageway. In an emergency you have to make your way to the door and jump out. There is a hatch on the top for water landing.

"On an aircraft carrier the helicopters launch first before the winged aircraft, then after the search and rescue helicopter is up, the E-2 Hawkeye is the first winged aircraft to launch. The fighter and bomber planes are faster so they can complete their mission more quickly, and return to the carrier," English said. "We often can fly our figure eight pattern and remain on station for hours monitoring events so we are generally the last to recover. In fact, there were times during Desert Storm where we would take off from the *Saratoga* in the Red Sea, fly our mission, and we actually would land in Saudi Arabia to refuel so we could get back to the *Saratoga*."

Establishing a stable flying pattern is essential for the radar to work optimally, English explained. "We had a few spots from the Red Sea towards the border of Saudi Arabia and Iraq where we would go maintain station there. You know you are on the flight schedule for the day and you are in your flight suit and you go to the ready room," English said describing a typical day at sea.

"In the ready room they have a briefing, which in a war-time mission is packed with all the other pilots and crew members. On big missions it is standing room only. So we, the E-2 crews, like crews of other aircraft, have to go through the maintenance book of the aircraft we're taking up to see if there are any issues from the previous flight and whether it is was properly fixed, and then you have to go up on deck to preflight the aircraft inside and outside, checking everything from the tires to the hydraulics, to the boxes inside and connections, and do the preflight checks that you normally do. The pilots and the NFOs have their own checklists. We wore a flight suit and helmet but inside the airplane are the parachutes and the life rafts connected to the seats. With the engines roaring we would be facing forward for the launch and then once in flight we would turn sideways to monitor the consoles for the mission. "

The United States was part of a coalition of Western countries arrayed against Saddam Hussein, and had set an ultimatum for him to leave Kuwait by January 17, 1991. "We as young junior officers thought he would back down."

When Hussein refused to leave by the deadline, the senior officers briefed us on the ship and told us we were

Lieutenant Commander Rick English in an E-2 Hawkeye.

going to go and it would start tomorrow. Wow, that was a surprise to us, but this is what we signed up to do."

The first night, according to English, "Our E-2 launched and we flew to our station and conducted our mission. It was somewhat the fog of war. We thought that we had lost communications with a couple of aircraft. When we landed back on the carrier we learned that we had lost two aircraft, an F-18 and an A-6. We know each other well enough from all the training we do with other squadrons. You knew most by name, or face or even voice over the radio. We later learned the crew of the A-6 that was shot down were taken as prisoners-of-war, but six months or so later were released during an exchange. An F-18 pilot was missing and we did not know what had

Rick English at the Office of Naval Intelligence.

happened to him. We knew where he was when we lost contact but we did not know if it was the result of a shoot down or mechanical problems. He was senior to me but we all knew each other.

"We later learned that Lieutenant Commander Michael Scott Speicher had been shot down and became the first American combat casualty of the war. His remains were not recovered until 2 August 2009; his fate had not been known until then. Even though we were successful, eventually the losses of our friends that first night made us somber and increased our need to focus." English served throughout the entire but brief Gulf War.

"I was due to leave the squadron and I took a job in D.C. with the Office of Naval Intelligence as an aviation intelligence analyst. I became an expert in certain countries and I would brief officers on what to expect if they went up against this particular country."

When English was getting ready to become a civilian again, there was a reduction in force and the Navy had a program called Troops to Teachers. He got a masters degree in education from Marymount College in Virginia as part of that program."

"During the cruise one of my buddies in the squadron who had married a girl from Scituate was showing pictures of his wife and family, and I asked him who one of them was and he said it was his wife's cousin, Jean Smith." English and Smith started corresponding while he was on the *Saratoga*. They met after coming back from the war cruise and married in 1993. Jean Smith is the daughter of Billy Smith, well known track and cross country coach at Scituate High School. In 1999, English and his wife relocated to Scituate, where she teaches at Wampatuk School and at Jenkins.

A TIME FOR WAR

The Buddy

Daniel Hanafin

I WAS SCOOTING DOWN—WITHIN THE SPEED LIMIT—First Parish Road in my son, John's, "hot rod," for which I am caretaker while he serves in Iraq with the Marines, when I spotted a big red white and blue sign in front of a house that read "Our Soldier is Home." My journalistic instincts told me there is a story here and I made a mental note to return.

The soldier in question was kind enough to grant me an interview. His name is Daniel Hanafin, life-long Scituate resident, who attained the rank of Eagle with Scituate's Scout Troop #90, and graduated from Scituate High School Class of '95.

"I joined the Marines right out of Scituate High School," Hanafin said.

There was something his mother had mentioned on the phone when I was setting up the interview—then it came to me.

"I understand you knew Coby Cutler?" I asked.

"He was my best friend through Scituate High School. We entered boot camp at Parris Island together on the same day. The Marines had a program then called 'the buddy program' where they would allow two best friends to team up so that you could serve together during your first enlistment if at all possible. Coby was my teammate."

Unfortunately, Coby Cutler, was tragically killed in an accident at Parris Island that August and is memorialized in Scituate's annual road run. The tragedy of Coby's untimely death has passed into Marine Corps and Scituate's history, leaving his buddy team member, his family, and so many others, to go on without him.

After completing boot camp, Hanafin decided to go on active duty and has been on it or in the active reserves ever since, specializing in combined heavy weapons and serving with, among other units, the Marines 3/8 Weapons Company. According to Hanafin, combined heavy weapons "are such things as TOW wire guided missiles that can be fired by one man, anti-tank guns, and machine guns." In other words, he's been a "grunt," slang for an infantryman, all these years.

During his military career, Hanafin has traveled far from home, and has been in "harm's way" more than a few times. Early in his military career he served with the Marine Guard Defense Force at the U.S. Base at Guantanamo, Cuba. He served in Japan and traveled to Alaska, Canada, and Norway, and trained with Allied forces. As events in the Balkans heated up, he participated in a U. S. Navy battle group patrolling the Mediterranean, which he referred to as the "Med float."

"Our unit was the first one into Albania where we served for about a month and a half, and then on to Kosovo."

According to Hanafin, after the "Med Float" he went from active duty to active reserves for a brief period, but early in 2000 he joined back on active duty for further training and travel.

Daniel Hanafin is welcomed home by his family.

"In September 2005, we got deployed to Camp Falujah, Iraq, which is located about fifteen miles from Baghdad. I served as a camp guard, as well as guard duty protecting water supplies serving the camp and nearby towns. This area was the major distribution center of the water supply infrastructure serving the local towns, some of which had no such water supply previously, and these pumping stations were very important to the people." Hanafin told me that the water supply system, which had been upgraded to serve more people, was always a potential target for terrorists.

While serving in Iraq, Hanafin also provided escort support for convoys traveling through the countryside and towns. This was hazardous duty requiring a watchful eye for such things as improvised explosive devices (IEDs) which were a constant menace and have been responsible for the deaths and injuries of so many American troops.

"When I was there, the morale of the Marines was good, and they were kept busy 24/7," Hanafin said. He completed his service in Iraq and returned home to be greeted by a large welcome sign put up in front of the house by his family.

Hanafin's dedicated service has paid off in his military career with promotions and additional responsibility. He is a staff sergeant (E-6), a section leader, responsible for anywhere from thirteen to twenty-six men.

Hanafin remains on active reserve status, and as the Marine Corps' mission changes, will be assigned to "a mobile assault platoon, or a now-forming unit of combined forces." In the meantime he will continue with further training in the reserves in preparation for possible activation to one of these new units. "[At any time,] I could be called up to serve where needed," Hanafin said.

During his thirteen years of service with the Marines, Hanafin admitted modestly that he has been awarded twenty-one ribbons and medals.

As to the way the media reports events in Iraq, Hanafin said, "The press is not giving the whole story on the reality of the war, [but rather what appears to be a] biased slant toward its own agenda regarding the war." Always the guardian, when Hanafin is not serving with the Marines, his civilian job is in security at Beth Israel Hospital in Boston.

At the end of the interview, sitting at the sun dappled picnic table with him, a sad nostalgic emotion mixed with pride descended upon me. He came home to a mother who hangs a blue star in the front window, a loving family who express their pride by having purchased not one, but two large welcome home signs (the other one hangs near Route 3, designed by the talented and creative Jesse Allen of Scituate's Harbor Sign Company). Hanafin came home to be near his buddy and the memories. Later when I reflected on Hanafin, I could not help but make the connection with Coby, these sons of Scituate, and the words of the poet Robert Louis Stevenson came to me:

Home is the sailor, home from the sea,
And the hunter home from the hill.

A TIME FOR WAR

"Chosen Soldier"

Major Tom Scanzillo

"Whom shall I send, and who will fight for us?" Then I said, "Here am I. Send me." —Isaiah - 6:8

E very citizen [in the United States] has been granted the desired freedom and material goods in such quantity and of such quality as to guarantee in theory the pursuit of happiness...So why and for what should one risk one's precious life in defense of common values and particularly in such nebulous cases when the security of one's nation must be defended in a distant country?" said Alexander Solzhenitsyn in a 1978 address at Harvard University.

Why indeed? And where do we get such citizens?

It was not so long ago that young Major Tom Scanzillo was a kid boogie boarding at Minot Beach. Today, he serves in that dark and deadly arena of small tactical operations on the front lines in those, according to Alexander Solzhenitsyn, "nebulous cases when the security of one's nation must be defended in a distant country."

Tom is a "Chosen Soldier," the name given to those selected to train as special forces warriors, as described in Dick Couch's 2008 book.

"I was raised in Scituate and attended its public schools. As soon as I graduated from Scituate High School, I entered the United States Military Academy. Upon graduation from West Point, I received a commission as a Second Lieutenant [2nd Lt.] in 1998."

Tom has always been motivated to excel, and his military career is no exception. After West Point Tom attended the Engineer Officer Basic Course at Ft. Leonard Wood, Missouri. His next assignment was to the Army's Jump School at Ft. Benning, Georgia, where he received his Airborne wings having completed five jumps from airplanes. The Army Ranger School was next. It is one of the most intense infantry combat tactics courses in all the military services for training in woodland, mountain, and swamp operations. Not surprisingly Tom completed the course the first time, without being "recycled"—as many are—at any of the three stages of the training cycle. He received the coveted Army Ranger Tab, a service school military decoration of the United States Army awarded to those relatively few who accept the challenge, and have the physical and mental stamina to complete the sixty-one day long course.

"It was essentially a test of how long you can stand being cold, wet, tired, and hungry, and continue to operate tactically on muscle memory alone," Tom said of the ordeal.

"I went to the 10th Mountain Division following Ranger School at Fort Drum in upstate New York. I served

Tom Scanzillo at the Al-F'tha Gap, Iraq, 2009

as a combat engineer platoon leader and with the sappers—breachers of fortifications, and enemy enclaves. Each infantry battalion in the 10th Mountain has an associated sapper platoon. We were in the infantry battalion at the same time as serving as engineers."

During his tour at Fort Drum, Tom deployed to Macedonia and Kosovo. "I was primarily responsible for working with NATO forces to de-mine roads and villages while there."

From Kosovo Tom was assigned to Fort Bragg for Special Forces Assessment and Selection, which is Phase I of Special Forces (Green Beret) training. "I was invited to attend Special Forces training after completing the month-long selection, but first had to attend the Captain's Career Course, which was the next step in Professional Military Education for officers. Following that I returned to Fort Bragg to complete Phases II though VI of the Special Forces Qualification Course." This multifaceted yearlong course, in addition to advanced small unit tactics and Special Operations leadership training, includes a language school, and an advanced Survival, Evasion, Resistance & Escape (SERE) program. From there he went on to earn his "HALO wings" at the elite High Altitude-Low Opening (HALO) military free fall school, and was subsequently assigned as the commander of a Special Forces Operational Detachment–Alpha (SFOD-A, or "A-Team") in 1st Special Forces Group (Airborne).

From his headquarters in Okinawa, Tom deployed to several other countries in the Far East including South Korea, Thailand, Indonesia, Malaysia and the Philippines, where he served in the Joint Special Operation Task Force Philippines, from 2004-2008 during Operation Enduring Freedom—Philippines (OEF-P). According to Tom, OEF-P though not widely known "is a major frontier in the worldwide counter-terrorism fight, and a model for multi-dimensional counter-insurgency operations." The task force worked throughout Mindanao and the Southern Philippines to locate, eliminate, and prevent the resurgence of radical Islamist non-state actors – like Jemm'ah Islamiy'ah and the Al-Qaida linked Abu Sayyaf Group –

primarily by building the capacity of the indigenous forces using a whole of government approach, in conjunction with the US Embassy and national interagency effort. Tom's team began as a "pilot team" – typically the first team to go into a difficult or hostile environment to conduct initial reconnaissance and shape the mission – and within months had incorporated operational elements of Civil Affairs, Psychological Operations, Air Force Special Tactics Teams, and Naval Special Warfare (SEALs). In the later years, Tom would round out his time in the Philippines as the Director of Operations for the 800-man Joint Special Operations Task Force. Years later, while working towards his Masters Degree, the US Naval War College would publish his case study on OEF-P and Influence Warfare and integrate it into the permanent curriculum at the college.

Shifting focus to the Middle East theater of operations, Tom took a team to Operation Iraqi Freedom advised an Iraqi Infantry Battalion and an Iraqi Border Patrol Battalion in all operations and aspects along 200 kilometers of the Iranian border. "I was a specialized team commander working with Iraqi forces in a national counterterrorism effort. Someone put this into perspective for me. You put an Iraqi battalion or brigade into the fight, and you bring an American battalion or brigade home. That's primarily the reason I volunteered to go there for a year." His team spent almost every day outside the wire with their Iraqi counterparts, and established a fully functional combat outpost on the border, which became the focal point for the US effort in the region. As the mission grew in scope, Tom led his team in integrating joint, combined and interagency operations between the coalition forces, Special Operations Forces, and the US multi-agency effort. Of the experience in Iraq, Tom said "keeping this team together was a daily challenge to my abilities as a leader, and the most rewarding part was fulfilling my vow to bring everyone home at the end. One of the most valuable lessons I learned here is that everyone can be set to good purpose, given the proper direction and some unconventional thinking."

Following his time in Iraq and subsequently the Naval War College, Tom was assigned to the 10th Special Forces Group in Colorado. During this tour, he deployed to several different countries in Africa to stand up and support operations against Joseph Kony and the Lord's Resistance Army in Central Africa, and al-Shabbab in East Africa. Upon redeployment he took command of the Special Forces Advanced Mountain Operations School in Colorado, where he was charged with the overall training and preparation of forces operating for long periods of time in high-altitude alpine terrain.

When prompted Tom admitted that he been awarded some decorations: Airborne wings, Air Assault wings, Military Free Fall "HALO" wings, the US Army Ranger tab, and his Green Beret. He has also earned the Combat Infantryman's Badge, and already has earned five and one half rows of ribbons, including two Bronze Stars.

As of this writing, the young major has served eight combat tours in various outposts on the frontiers of freedom and when asked if he would continue to make the Army his career, said, "Frankly, I didn't expect to be in this long. I did not expect to be in the running to become a Lieutenant Colonel in Army Special Forces."

Of his military career to this point Tom said, "It has been challenging and rewarding my entire time. The direction we are taking things in all these countries is productive and important. We are seeing people take ownership of their own governments and their own political issues. One of the major aspects is working at the people level. We're essentially giving people alternative options to supporting the radicals and insurgents, who have no viable options for providing safety and stability. Our presence is helping these governments provide the people with education and the tools for good governance."

Tom is currently assigned to US Army Special Forces Command, and (when not deployed overseas) works between Fort Bragg, the Pentagon, and multiple commands in the National Capitol Region.

A TIME FOR WAR

Letter from Bethesda

Jamil Brown

I RECEIVED A LETTER IN THE FORM OF AN E-MAIL from a recently wounded Marine sergeant who was medevac'd from Iraq to the National Naval Medical Center in Bethesda, Maryland. Incidentally, the word "Bethesda" is particularly apt for a hospital, because it means in Hebrew "the house of Mercy." Although I have never met this young Marine, who is from Dorchester, his e-mail was in response to an e-mail that I had sent him. But to understand its meaning to me, it is necessary to flash back about three weeks ago to Iraq.

Three Marines were on a night mission in a Humvee, the sergeant from Dorchester was manning the radio and was in communication with another Marine, who happens to be from Scituate, and who was at the headquarters base, not far from Fallujah. They are not only colleagues but friends. Some nights the Scituate Marine went out in the Humvee to man the radio, but this was his night for radio watch at headquarters.

Suddenly, and in the midst of their radio communication, the Marine from Scituate heard a loud explosion, followed

Marine Sergeant Jamil Brown at Logan Airport, Boston, receiving a welcome home hero's return. (*Photo courtesy Boston Herald*)

by silence. Instinctively, he knew what had happened. The Humvee had hit an Improvised Explosive Device (IED). He called in the medevac and directed the chopper to the site. He had no idea if any of his buddies on board had survived the blast. After calling in the medevac, all he could do was wait by the radio, listen, and pray. Only later would he learn that they all had survived, but with serious injuries. When the Scituate Marine later called his parents, he tried to disguise it, but they knew that the memory of that incident still weighed heavily on him. The medics had told him of the severity of the wounds to his sergeant—which included the loss of his foot and other injuries, including to his arm—and of the injuries to his other buddies. Before this incident he had already lost two of his pals and fellow Marines.

When she heard about this incident, the Scituate Marine's mother got the sergeant's name and found out he had already been medevac'd to Bethesda. She followed this up with a call to Bethesda Naval Medical Center to ask his caregivers how he was doing, so she could communicate that information to her son in Iraq. To her surprise, she was connected directly to the sergeant. Later, she reported the conversation and that he sounded good, in spite of his serious injuries, and that he would like to have visitors. She mentioned to the sergeant she had heard that her son was the last person he was speaking with before the incident. The sergeant remarked that this information sparked his memory, which he is still recovering. I subsequently got his e-mail address, followed-up her phone call with an e-mail, and he responded in the same manner. I would like to share his e-mail with you.. Although he wasn't thinking of it ever getting published when he wrote it, he has no objections.

Mr. Wheatley:

I hope I'm not being too formal, it's just habit. It's [the spelling of my name] actually Jamil, but that's okay, very few people get the name right. I know that John has mentioned my name to you guys before, but I was unaware that I made such an impression on him. As an NCO, you, [know]. Well, until his mother called me, I didn't remember being on the radio with him. I[t] was like popping a bubble, and the memory came back. I know why he tried to cover it up, even after he was able to tell you. He was afraid. Some he knew closely and maybe admired, someone he would shoot the [bull] with, just got blown up, and he was there on the radio to hear the blast! As long as he's all right now....Corresponding electronically is not a hindrance, just bear with me on responding. My right arm was damaged. It is healing up, but I don't have full range of motion, so I can't type as fast as I used to. Thanks for your kind words. It always amazes me how many people care. Lying in this bed, it's hard for me do anything. Having so many people call and visit me keeps my spirits up...I am at your service....Thanks again for your kindness, and I am proud to serve this nation.

Semper Fi.

Jamil Brown.

Purple Hearts and Blue Star Moms

Maura McGowan Yanosick

ONCE LEARNING OF MY SON'S DEPLOYMENT, I began looking for local support for military parents, and I was surprised to find that there were no chapters of the Blue Star Mothers in the State of Massachusetts," said Mrs. Maura McGowan Yanosick of Scituate.

According to an article posted on the Blue Star Mothers website, the Blue Star flag is hung in the windows of homes who have a loved one serving in the armed forces, particularly during times of war.

According to www.usflag.org: "The Blue Star flag was designed and patented by World War I Army Capt. Robert L. Queissner of the 5th Ohio Infantry who had two sons serving on the front line. This flag quickly became the unofficial symbol of a child in service…On Sept. 24, 1917, an Ohio congressman read the following into the Congressional Record: '…The mayor of Cleveland, the Chamber of Commerce, and the governor of Ohio have adopted this service flag. The world should know of those who give so much for liberty. The dearest thing in all the world to a father and mother—their children…' Also during World War I, the blue star became gold if a service member was killed or died on active duty. The Gold Star Mothers of America, Inc. came from this group."

The notice that Yanosick's son, Justin, a member of the U.S. Army National Guard, would be deployed for his third tour in August 2006 was the stimulus for Yanosick to act. She did her research and began the process of chartering a local Blue Star Mothers chapter for eastern Massachusetts.

However, two months into her initiation of the chartering process for the first Chapter of the Blue Star Mothers in the State, Yanosick learned that Chapter One of the Blue Star Mothers had recently been founded in Leominster, Massachusetts. Undeterred, Yanosick's efforts soon succeeded with her chartering Chapter Two of the Blue Star Mothers for Eastern Massachusetts, (EMAC) in September 2006 here in Scituate. As the EMAC website states: "…our Chapter has rapidly grown to 60 plus members and associate members. The Chapter has engaged with local Veterans and civic organizations to work with them in supporting our service men and women."

"The Chapter has a threefold mission: we support our service members [and their families]; veterans in our communities, and support each other," said Yanosick. To this end Scituate's Blue Star Mothers Chapter has sent more than one hundred and seventy care packages to deployed troops, personally delivered care packages

Maura Yanosick standing in the Massachusetts Military
Heroes Fund Memorial Garden of Flags on Boston
Common with two of her grandchildren, Patrick and
Mallory.

to hospitalized veterans at the West Roxbury Veterans
Administration Hospital, and has sent numerous cards to
troops and veterans.

Yanosick observed that the Scituate Chapter sent
handmade Mothers' Day cards to the troops deployed so
that they could send them to their mothers on that special
day. "One of our Mother's Day cards was sent to a soldier
who was subsequently killed in action. At the services, the
mother of the deceased soldier told me that her son had

written her that the card had brought him much comfort," Yanosick said. Members of the Scituate's Blue Star Mothers Chapter have attended thirteen services for soldiers on the South Shore who were killed in action. "We also have a Blue to Gold Star transition program where we present families with the Gold Star," Yanosick said.

"We sponsored a service day through Dogs for Deaf and Disabled Americans' (NEADS) new Canine for Combat Veterans program...at the assistant dogs' graduation at Hynes Auditorium in Boston. Our Buy a Bone campaign has raised nearly $7,000.00. Our puppy's name is 'Star,'" she said. "The trained dog will be given to the next combat veteran candidate." Yanosick noted that the $7,000.00 will be donated to help defray the $10,000.00 responsibility assumed by the dog's new owner, which is only part of the $40,000.00 cost of raising and training these special dogs.

"We have [regular] meetings for members and interested veterans and their families with guest speakers who address such things as Post Traumatic Stress Syndrome [PSTD]," and other issues of interest to recently returned veterans and their families.

Yanosick, who grew up in Scituate, is married to Richard "Rick" Yanosick, an EMT and member of the Scituate Fire Department. They have been married twenty-four years and are the parents of three children: Justin, age twenty-three; Cara, age twenty; and Meg, sixteen.

Yanosick is a graduate of Bridgewater State College, class of '83, with an Education major. She taught for years at the Erdman pre-school in Scituate; she has also taught in the Abington Public Schools as an Orton Gillingham

Specialist. She presently serves as the Child and Youth Coordinator for the Massachusetts Family of the Massachusetts National Guard. In this capacity, Yanosick supports Massachusetts National Guard members and their families with pre-deployment, deployment, and re-integration programs, including such things as subsidized child care, educational support liaison for students of deployed families, coordinating regional events, as well as leadership training of National Guard youth statewide.

The Eastern Chapter of Blue Star Mothers is an IRS Section 501.c3 charitable corporation, and receives no funds, other than donations. The chapter's website is http://www.bluestarmothers-emac.org/home.html.

Yanosick is also a regular volunteer with other non-profits who assist veterans and military families including: Homes for Our Troops (HSFOT), Massachusetts Military Heroes Fund (MMHF), the Brockton VA, the Achilles Freedom Team, and the Jeffrey Coombs Memorial Foundation.

A TIME FOR WAR

Reunion

John Wheatley

IN THE FRIDAY, OCTOBER 27, 2006 EDITION OF THE *Patriot Ledger,* in an article slugged "A Home Coming For Heroes," and subtitled "South Shore Marines are back from Iraq," the article states, in part, of the glorious occasion, "...at least one Marine each came home to Abington, Braintree, Canton, Cohasset, Halifax, Hanson, Hingham, Holbrook, Hull, Kingston, Milton, Norwell, Plymouth, Quincy, Stoughton, Weymouth and Whitman." If I may be so proud, dear reader, of my son and my home town, I suggest that Scituate be added to this Honor Role of Towns on the South Shore.

All week long prior to the homecoming, which occurred on Thursday, October 26th, the Marine Corps moms were clogging the phone lines trying to get a fix on when the 1st Battalion of the 25th Marine Regiment, New England's only and storied Reserve Unit, would return home.

The night before the reunion, the phone rang, and Marine Mom Colleen said, "They will arrive at Devens at 7 a.m. Plan to be there early." In order to get to Devens by 6:30 A.M., we left the house at 3:30 A.M., picked up Gary Vitty, who joined us as an unofficial representative of Scituate's American Legion Post #144. We drove the two hours or so and still arrived in the dark. Anxious families were milling about the dark parking lot braving a cold brisk wind asking each other where the ceremonies were to take place. Ever so gradually the sky was brightening, and there was blessedly no rain.

At seven the cadre stationed at Devens opened a building where we could all convene, and warm up. There was a lecture about Post Traumatic Stress Disorder, and the signs families should be aware of. Then the word came down in the typical military manner of "Hurry Up and Wait —the Marines won't arrive until 10;00 A.M." It was during this period when we were all waiting in the room—most of us strangers to one another—that we became part of one big family held together by a common bond. Our sons, daughters, fathers, brothers, sisters, were coming home. We shared stories as we waited. Some went outside with big posters and ladders to decorate the side of the building that the Marines would see when they faced the cheering crowd.

The time flew and before we knew it we were told they would arrive in fifteen minutes. We assembled outside. The cool breeze tousled our hair, but the sun was bright as we gathered on a grassy staging area. We could not have asked for a better day weather-wise. Devens cadre personnel held back the surging crowd in the still large empty field beyond. The television news reporters swept the exuberant crowd, and each time they focused on one particular section, they were met with a spontaneous eruption of

John Wheatley in Iraq.

cheers of joy and relief. Finally people started pointing, "There they are!" Far off in the distance a caravan of buses slowly approached. It seemed like an eternity waiting, but finally we were rewarded by the first glimpse of the American flag and Marine Corp flag moving slowly and high up near the side of the field. The color guard led the Marines marching smartly in formation wearing their dessert camouflage fatigues, hats and desert boots. They marched right by as if not even aware of the screaming crowd. Then the officer leading the march shouted, "Halt." Orders were barked, but we could not understand them. We heard another bark, and the battalion, as if one person, did a smart left face, and we were looking right at them from a distance of about 100 feet. People were straining to pick out their loved one from all these men and women dressed alike.

They stood at attention and in silence for about two minutes. Thankfully, there were no speeches. Everyone just wanted the reunion, and then to take their Marine home. Another bark, and suddenly they all loosened up and started walking toward us. People rushed the Marines. There were mothers with young children and babies in their arms running to welcome Dad home. There were tears, but they were tears of joy. I spotted my son, John, and my wife and I and Gary Vitty rushed to give him a hug. It was a wonderful, glorious day—a day that no one who was there to greet a loved one will ever forget as long as he lives.

As we passed back toward the building, I noticed a row of simple wooden stakes planted in the grass. Each one had an eight and a half inch sized placard with a picture and little biography of one of the eleven of the Battalion who did not return. Amidst all the joy, there was sadness too. There was one more Marine who would have been there could she have made it, and that was former State Representative Mary Jeanette Murray, a Marine herself, who had passed earlier in the week.

Wreaths Across Scituate

Karen Kelley

A FLAG FLAPPING ARCTIC WIND MOCKED THE bright sun spangled Veterans Memorial on the Common on Saturday, December 13, as Scituate Gold Star mother Karen Kelley stood on the monument pedestal to address the small gathering of town residents and dignitaries as part of a hastily organized Scituate participation in the "Wreaths across America/Arlington Project."

"I stood up there and I was so emotionally overcome that I just wasn't able to continue. I didn't plan to break down," Karen Kelley said. Still more frustrating for Kelley was that she was unable to deliver her message. What was that undelivered message? But first some background.

Michael J. Kelley was one of four children of Joe and Karen. "He was baptized at Christ's Lutheran Church in Scituate. Our minister said of young Michael, 'God help you, Karen, he's going to be a 'hellion' to raise but he's going to turn out like me.' As he was growing up he would in fact imitate the minister. He was raised in a family where God was first, then family and then 'me,'"

Kelley said. "Mike was a reader. When he was growing up he loved to read and play with his Legos."

"He loved baseball," but a beaning at Little League ended his baseball career. "While at Scituate High School (SHS), Mike played soccer and in his senior year received the most improved player award. Michael had an artistic/creative talent. He studied art and poetry at SHS. All my other children—Shawn, Kari and Colleen—were in the musical department there."

Michael graduated from SHS in June of 1997. In the fall of that year he joined the National Guard. As a member of the Massachusetts National Guard "Mike's training took him all across America," his mother said. "He did basic in South Carolina. We drove to his graduation."

From basic Michael went to Fort Huachuca, Arizona, for seven months for Army Intelligence training. "That's near where he got his little leprechaun tattoo," Kelley said. Following that Michael returned to Scituate to serve as a "Weekend Warrior" out of the Quincy Armory and worked for a landscaping company in his civilian job.

In March of 1999, in light of their pastor's prediction, the Kelleys were not surprised that Michael was selected for more training at the Army's Chaplain School as a chaplain's assistant. After Chaplain School, Michael came back to Scituate to serve with his National Guard unit. "He was over six feet tall, but he had small hands and he was very good at mechanical things such as wiring," Karen Kelley said.

"When 9/11 hit they were all put on alert and he was activated to homeland defense serving out of Camp Edwards. He was transferred to the Rehoboth Armory," Kelley recalled. According to Kelley, when the Quincy

Joe and Karen Kelley at the dedication of the Michael J. Kelley Tactical Training Center at Camp Edwards named in honor of their son.

Guard was deployed to Iraq, Mike was one of eight out of the Rehoboth unit who volunteered for a special mission to Afghanistan.

"Michael was home for Christmas of 2005. He left this house January 3 of 2005 to go to Fort Sill. The day he left here we had a special breakfast," Kelley said, taking out a larger than life sized homemade postcard with a picture of Mike with family members. "I put on a blue star and wrote Michael J. Kelley, God Bless you, keep your eyes on the star, faith, hope and love."

Deployed from Ft. Sill directly to Afghanistan on April 1, 2006, "Mike called from there in May giving us a list of things that they needed to secure their little hut. One thing he wanted was canned foam to fill the holes and keep the sand out. After that, we got a few phone calls and e-mails. His last phone call home was June 6, 2006, and he said, 'Hi, mom…I still haven't got my packages.' So we went to buy it all again. On June 8, 2006, I was babysitting my Kari's baby daughter, Olivia, in Rockland. I was reading the just delivered *Patriot Ledger* and I saw a story headlined 'Two killed in Afghanistan.' The first thing I did was to pray."

Late that night around 11:15, I was in bed and then the police car pulled up in front of the house escorting the Army car. I jumped up out of bed and the Army officers were standing there with Joe. 'I am sorry to inform you that you son was killed,' the Army chaplain said."

"Last Saturday, as I was making my way to the memorial I heard behind me, 'Hi, Mom.' It was what Michael used to say. I was trying to get composure to give the speech I had prepared entitled 'How we pulled this miracle off [the Arlington Wreath Project/Wreaths Across America] in so short a time.' How it began was around Thanksgiving my daughter, Kari, found it on the website, called me about it, and I talked to Ed Covell, commander of Scituate American Legion Post #144, and then to Scituate Veterans agent Gary Carlo.

"My message prepared for the wreaths ceremony was our family was looking to do something in the community in Michael's name, but also something to serve as a thank you for all the support we have had—an annual event with whatever funds raised were to be for families of veterans. We started with seven wreaths and it became a goal of the Kelleys to obtain 350 decorated wreaths." As part of the ceremony that day about 360 wreaths were placed that day on the graves at Cudworth.

A TIME FOR WAR

The Last Full Measure of Devotion

Michael Kelley

"THE SECOND CALL I GOT FROM MICHAEL WAS THE LAST one," his mom Karen Kelley said. "It was two days before he died and it was our longest conversation of the two calls he had made to me. He said he was getting acclimated. He wanted to know if I had sent him the supplies from the list he had given me during his first call a month or so before, since he had not received it yet. He had a new list and a question: 'Mom, what did you teach me about fish?' and I said if it smells like fish, don't eat the fish. 'Okay, I am going to tell all my buddies.' He was always concerned about the other soldiers." Kelley knew she could not ask questions.

"That conversation was the best I ever had with him," she said. "At least he was able to say, 'I love you and goodbye.' Two days later, on June 8, 2005, I read that two soldiers had been killed in Shkin, Afghanistan. I said my prayers. I was babysitting my granddaughter, Olivia, and this was probably around one in the afternoon. At 11:15

that night the Army's casualty officer and the Chaplain were at my door."

Michael Kelley was born in Weymouth on September 2, 1978 at South Shore Hospital. His parents, Joe and Karen Kelley, were not "townies" but had relocated from Brockton to Scituate forty-three years earlier. Michael was the third child of the Kelleys, the oldest being his brother Shawn (44), and sisters Karianne (41) and Colleen (30). Michael would have celebrated his 37th birthday on Sept 2, 2015.

Michael Kelley attended Scituate public schools— Cushing Elementary School, Gates Middle School, and Scituate High School. After high school he attended Bridgewater State College but did not graduate.

According to his parents Michael's interest were reading, art, Legos, soccer, computers, and the challenges of computer games. From an early age he loved drawing and also writing short stories. Then in high school he expressed an interest in writing a book and doing the illustrations.

In high school, Michael was like a lot of kids his age, not sure of what he wanted to do when he graduated in June of 1997. "To give him some direction, I thought it might be a good idea to introduce him to the Massachusetts National Guard," his father, Joe Kelley, said. "There was a recruiting station in Hyannis and I took him down there. He signed up the same day."

"I was not happy about it," Karen Kelley said. "I saw Michael in a different light, because I spent the most time with him. I saw him as a very creative child, not like his older brother who had gone to college and became an engineer."

Although she was not "happy" with the surprise enlistment, Karen Kelley did not fight it. "After he

Sergeant Michael Kelley

signed up, the recruiter came to the house, and I dealt with the recruiter," Michael's mother said. "He thanked me for being the organized mother since I had all of Michael's medical records which the Guard required."

Three months after enlisting, in January of 1998, Michael left Scituate for Ft. Jackson, South Carolina for Army basic training and completed the program in March. From there he received orders to Ft. Huachuca, Arizona, for specialized training.

"He came home to Scituate for Thanksgiving 1998," Karen Kelley recalled, and then was assigned to the Quincy Massachusetts Armory where he attended drills on weekends. While serving in the Guard, when not doing drills, he worked at the local Village Market and J. Michael Landscaping. His last place of employment was Nextel, selling cell phones, and he attended Bridgewater State College part-time where he was taking writing and art courses.

"He wanted to write books. He had done a couple of children's books for friends. He always had a smile," his dad said.

According to his parents, when 9/11 hit he started writing a personal journal. He knew he was being activated, but not sure when.

"Then a few days after 9/11 he came rushing home from work and said, 'Mom, I have been activated and I have to report to Camp Edwards," Karen said. Soon after that, he left Camp Edwards on the Cape where he served as a security guard,

"He served there until April 2003," Karen Kelley said.

While serving at Camp Edwards his Quincy unit was activated to be deployed to Iraq. His mission on the Cape ended and he was reassigned to the Rehoboth Armory were Michael volunteered to go to Afghanistan.

He left January 3, 2005 for Ft. Sill, Oklahoma where he would be assigned to a tactical acquisition battery.

"He trained to be part of a an eight-man crew manning a portable radar unit in the field designed to acquire the direction and location of incoming fire for return fire by our howitzer batteries," Joe Kelley said. "He was in Ft. Sill from Jan 3, 2005 until the end of March. On April 1, 2005 he was deployed to Afghanistan."

Kelley was sent to Shkin, Afghanistan, located on the Pakistan border. It was considered as the Army Special Forces forward operation base (FBO) and was nicknamed

"The Alamo." From there they would operate out on three week missions to outlying fire base locations where they would set up the portable batteries at these outposts and return to fire base Alamo.

"We did talk to Michael five times while he was in Afghanistan. On the first of the two calls he gave us a list of supplies that he and his buddies needed. One of the things on the list was spray can insulation. Michael said he needed it to keep out the sand from the equipment, and keeping the giant camel spiders from where they slept. "Oh, and they needed toilet paper," Karen said.

On June 8, 2005, Michael and another solder, U.S. Army Private First Class Emmanuel Hernandez from Puerto Rico, were killed while unloading a Chinook helicopter at a landing zone (LZ) whenthey came under attack from rocket fire. Several others were injured during the attack.

"The Casualty Officer informed us that Michael could be buried at one of several locations including Arlington National Cemetery," Karen said. "I said, 'Michael's coming home and he will be buried in Cudworth,'" the closest veterans cemetery in town to the Kelley home.

The funeral was held at Christ Lutheran Church in Scituate and attended by an overflow crowd. "So many military people offered to help us at the wake and they are still with us ten years later. They never forgot; they supported us all along. Whatever the Guard representatives promised to do, they did," Joe Kelley said.

Michael Kelley was the first Massachusetts Army National guardsman to be killed in action post 9/11 in Afghanistan and Iraq.

"In March of 2006, I went to see our state representative, who at the time was Frank Hynes, and said I want to do something to honor the memory of Michael. The bridge was an idea that came from the family.

"I said, 'Frank, I would like to do something big in Michael's honor.'

'What were you thinking?' Frank wanted to know.

'You know the bridge that goes over the North River? There is no name on it. [The bridge had been rebuilt in November 2001 on a section of highway that connects Scituate and Marshfield and places south.] What do we have to do to get that bridge named in Michael's honor?' And Representative Hynes said, 'I'll introduce a bill in the legislature to rename the bridge in his honor.'"

The bill easily passed the legislature and Governor Mitt Romney signed it on May 5, 2006. At the official dedication of the bridge, Michael's unit had just returned from Afghanistan. A contingent from the Massachusetts Army National Guard 101st Field Artillery fired a volley cannon salute. In addition, two F-16s that had been dispatched from Otis Air Force base to fly cover right after 9/11 flew in from the ocean, up the river, and over the bridge in tribute.

"It was healing for all who attended, especially those members of the Massachusetts Army National Guard that represented the Quincy and Rehoboth armories, where Michael served," Joe Kelley said.

In the spring of 2007, the Kelleys received a letter from Adjutant General Joseph Carter of the Massachusetts

Sergeant Michael Kelley (*right*) at Ft. Sill finishing up training just
before being deployed to Afghanistan.

National Guard that the Guard was establishing a training
center on the Cape and would they mind if they named it
after Michael. "Of course, we were honored," Karen Kelley
said.

The Kelleys were the guests of honor at the opening
ceremony presided over by the base commander, Brigadier
General Thomas Sellars. It was now to be knows as the
Sergeant Michael J. Kelley Tactical Training Base.

The tactical training base is designed to cut down the
danger time during the initial period of deployment when
troops are most vulnerable. "And it is working," Joe Kelley

said. "When Michael was killed he had been there sixty-nine days. Now that greatest threat period is down from one hundred days to thirty-five days."

In December 2008 the Kelleys had an opportunity to introduce "Wreathes Across America" to Scituate on the second Saturday of December.

"So Karen and I called Ed Covell, Commander of Scituate American Legion Post 144, and they were enthusiastic to lend support," Joe said. "After the successful initiation of the program to Scituate, I said to Ed, 'You guys did a tremendous job and I would like you to take it on as a mission.' So now part of their fundraising every year goes to the 'Wreathes Across America.' Is the Legion still part of it? Yes, absolutely they are part of it. Over the years, then-Commander Covell and subsequent commanders have asked me to participate in the town events on Memorial Day, Fourth of July, and Veterans Day. When my Mike was killed, Ed and his wife Lorraine were right at the door."

Shortly after Christmas of 2011 the Kelleys received a call from the editor of the *Scituate Mariner*, Nancy White. "She said, 'What's your thoughts on the school?'" Joe Kelley said.

"What school?" Joe asked.

"The school that the Massachusetts Army National Guard built in Michael's honor."

"I said, 'Tell me more.' She said, 'I just got it off the wire and I would like your response to it'

"All I got to say is that is one heck of a Christmas present for our family to receive," Joe Kelley said.

The challenge for the Kelleys now is to keep raising

funds for the school. One of the ways they are doing this is by teaming up with the Scituate Rotary Club # 4950, which has its own school support program in raising funds for Razia Jan and the "Razia's Ray of Hope Foundation." Razia Jan is the founder of the Zabuli Education Center, and has worked for many years to forge connections between Afghans and Americans.

"So our mission is to keep Michael's memory alive for what he stood for and what he died for," Joe and Karen Kelley said.

A TIME FOR WAR

Born to be a Marine

Coby Cutler

O NE THING I REGRET IS THAT DURING MY DAYS writing my column "Calling All Veterans," there were so many veterans in town that I did not interview. I got my ideas of potential interviewees from people in town who had read my column and would say to me, "You have to interview so-and-so who has a great story." And I would call the person, introduce myself and offer to interview them. Often, but not always, they would agree. But there is another category of veterans I did not interview and these were young men or women, high school students, who weren't veterans, but were in the process of enlisting, or planning to.

Coby Cutler was one of those. So, I wondered how do I fill a void when one of those yet-to-be veteran's service in the military ends up with a compelling story and is not around to tell it? I came to the conclusion that I would do the next best thing: interview the parents if they agreed and believed it might contribute to preserving, in this case, a son's memory.

One such couple was Quincie Ann Cutler, also know as "Q," and and Richard Cutler, also known as "Rick."

"Coby was born at Boston Hospital on April 17, 1977 when we were living in Scituate. Coby is our only child," Quincie said. "Rick was in the auto industry so we moved from Scituate to Detroit for about a year and from there to Pittsburgh, and back to Scituate when Coby was in the first grade."

When they first returned to Scituate their son attended Wampatuck Elementary School, but soon the family bought a house more convenient to another neighborhood school, Hatherly Elementary School. "Coby went through the Scituate Public School system, and graduated from Scituate High School in June of 1995," Quincie said.

Like many high school kids, Coby found he had a special interest. "Coby loved to cook," Rick said. "He was accepted to Johnson & Wales University Culinary Arts Institute in Rhode Island while still in high school. He saved a lot of money while in high school from his part-time jobs including as a line cook at the Red Lion Inn located in the next town over, Cohasset, but he had the Marine Corps in the back of his mind all along."

Coby's mother recalled an incident from Coby's early childhood that was a life-changing event. "When we lived in a very 'neighborhoody' place about twenty miles north of Pittsburgh, one of our friends had a red baseball cap with the gold Marine Corps logo on it, and he put it on Coby's head. And that hat never came off his head; he simply loved it. And it was Marine, Marine, Marine after that...and it became more intense in high

Coby Cutler

school. There he met Dan Hannifin who was also aspiring to the Marine Corps. They became great friends in high school."

Meanwhile, Coby was busy with outside work while a high school student, especially cooking to earn extra money. And he still had time to play Little League baseball as a pitcher and later in high school as a catcher. According to his mother, another influence on Coby was his two older cousins, Jonathan and Jeremy Richard, who preceded him in high school. Jonathan entered the

Marine Corps following his graduation from Scituate High School.

Coby and Dan Hannifin formed a plan while in high school to pre enlist in the Marine Corps under a then existent Marine Corps "Buddy program," where pals could sign up to go through boot camp together.

"Richard and I, having grown up in the '60s, were somewhat anti-military and we were trying to steer him more toward Johnson & Wales University first. Unbeknownst to us, Coby had already talked to a Marine recruiter, Sgt. Mark Bragdon, who he persuaded to call us. Sgt. Bragdon came to the house three times with several thick books all about the Marine Corps, and all about how the Marine Corps would help Coby. They wooed us and Coby wooed us, and we agreed that if he wants it that bad we're going to support this kid in what he wants to do."

During Coby's senior year the Cutler's signed a Marine Corps form granting permission for Coby to join the pre-enlistment program where he would train once a month on weekends at the base on the Cape.

It was in the spring of senior year that students have to fulfill so many hours of community service in order to graduate. But this extracurricular activity, combined with his cooking job, was getting in the way of the high school's community service requirement.

"I hounded him about it," Coby's mother said, "and told him if you don't finish your community service you are not going to graduate and if you don't graduate, you don't go into the Marine Corps. Well, nothing was being done so I picked up the phone and called his Sgt.

Bragdon, in Plymouth, and told him we were having a bit of a problem with Coby's community hours service requirement at the high hchool. He told me, 'Mrs. Cutler, don't worry about it, I will take care of it.'"

Quincie paused as she remembered the events. "Shortly thereafter, Coby called me at work. He said, 'Mom, Sergeant Bragdon called and wants to see me about my community hours.' And that day when I got home from work, Coby was there and he sort of had this wry little smile on his face—he had these big blue eyes and they just sparkled—and he said, 'My community service will be done.' I can still see the look on his face that day. I think he sort of knew that I had spoken with Sgt. Bragdon, but didn't say anything."

Marine Corps representatives in full dress uniform attended Coby's and Dan's graduation. The students were in cap and gown and on his cap Coby had a Marine Corps sticker. "Before Coby left for the Marine Corps he had his savings account from all of his part-time work as line cook, mowing lawns, and stuffing envelopes for a marketing company, and he was wondering what to do with it.

"I suggested we could split buying a car and he said no, that it would just sit here for four years, so I suggested why don't you put your money to work for you. So he made an appointment with a financial advisor at A.G. Edwards to help him invest the $10,000.00 he had saved in high school before he left for the Boot Camp."

That summer, in July of 1995, Coby Cutler and Dan Hannifin went to boot camp at Paris Island, South Carolina, together as buddies in the Marine Corps' buddy program, arriving on July 17, 1995.

"He became a squad leader right away, and in one letter we got from him he said, 'Mom, you don't have to make your letters so long, I hardly have time to eat.'"

Five and a half weeks later, while on the rifle range at Paris Island, a bolt of lightening struck and killed eighteen-year-old Coby.

"Ricky was in California on business and I came home from work, and right after I got into the house two Marine officers were at the door. They told me that Coby had died—struck by lightening," Quincie said. Two other Marines were injured, but they survived.

An overflow crowd attended Coby's funeral at Scituate's First Trinitarian Congregational Church where Marines in full dress uniform filled two pews, including the two Marines who recruited Coby and Dan Hannifin, Sgt. Mark Bragdon and Gunnery Sgt. Bill Bush.

A graveside service followed at nearby Mount Hope Cemetery where Coby was buried with full military honors, Marine rifle salute, taps, and the presentation of the folded flag to Coby's mother. Dan Hannifin, still a recruit at boot camp, had been granted leave to attend. They entered the Marines as part of the "Buddy System" and the Marines honored that promise to the end.

Scituate and the Marine Corps honored Coby's memory by hosting an annual 5K road race known as "Coby's Run" for seven years, using the money raised from that to build a new fitness center called the "The Coby Cutler Fitness Center" in Scituate High School.

SECTION EIGHT

9/11

A TIME FOR WAR

Walking in Sacred Dust

Mark DeLuca

"IT WAS BETWEEN 9:30 AND 10:00 A.M. WHEN I called Hayden because I had to go up to my town manager, Rocco Longo, to get permission from him to take volunteers from my department. I put out a call that anyone who wanted to come up on a voluntary basis, we are leaving this afternoon," said Cohasset Chief of Police Mark DeLuca who at the time was serving as Chief of Police of Duxbury.

When Assistant General Manager for Safety for the MBTA Robert Hayden's phone rang he had just arrived at the MBTA headquarters at Park Plaza in Boston to huddle with others watching the Twin Towers being hit by an aircraft. It was about 9:15 a.m. on September 11, 2001. Hayden and DeLuca are lifelong friends who had served together on the Boston Police Department.

"Chief DeLuca said that he was organizing a group of responders—first responders—to go to New York City and he was asking for volunteers," said Hayden who

Rescue workers on "the pile" at Ground Zero.

lives in Hingham. "He said he needed ten to twelve officers to go and he asked me if I would like to join them. He said we will be doing first aid, looking for bodies, doing anything to help the New York City Police Department and Fire Department. So I drove home, put on a pair of dungarees and sweatshirt, brought a toothbrush. I told my wife I was going; I did not know for how long, and drove to Duxbury in time to join the group that Mark had assembled."

"Bob was the first guy I called and all he asked was when are you leaving?" said DeLuca.

Insuring that Duxbury had adequate coverage, DeLuca found three police cruisers that were not going to be used. "We got up there in two and half hours— lights and sirens from Duxbury to New York—and arrived around 8:30 p.m.," DeLuca said. Both men vividly recall as they were approaching New York seeing a portable lighted sign with the chilling notice "NYC Closed." They were directed by emergency personnel to a holding area in New Jersey.

"We went in there and joined about 500 people— mostly fire and policemen. We learned that this was a holding pool of volunteers to be used as they were needed. After about twenty minutes, Chief DeLuca said, 'This isn't what we came to New York City for—let's go,'" said Hayden. "Chief DeLuca was the hero to me. When we were at that holding area in New Jersey, it takes a special person to say I'm not sitting here any longer; I am not going back to Boston and just get up and say, 'Let's go men.'"

But obstacles remained. As they drove deeper into the City they began to encounter manned wooden barricades.

"We were not supposed to drive into New York City, but our cars were marked Duxbury Police and they had blue lights on them. So the chief told everyone to turn on their blue lights and we drove straight by everyone who said stop, and in a very short time we came to ground zero. As we got closer I could see that there was a horrible pall of white dust that covered everything. This was around midnight. You breathed it, and it was on your hands," Hayden recalled.

The team could go no farther in the cars when they neared the actual site.

"The first thing I noticed was the New York City police cars just totally flattened. You could see abandoned vehicles. It was like a horror movie, like a Mad Max movie when there is nothing alive. You could not see more than one hundred feet—shadowy figures moved in the distance. Fire engines were flattened," said Hayden.

From the police cars the team trudged through the six inch deep powdery dust toward the shadowy figures.

"We got right up to the edge of this huge mound of destruction and there were probably a thousand people there who had already started working. There was no one in charge but there really did not have to be. There were lines about an eighth of a mile long where the workers were passing debris, pieces of steel, heavy concrete, from right to left," said Hayden.

The volunteers had assembled on top of the mound of destruction and DeLuca's team joined the line.

"You'd stand in the line and something would come to you and you would pass it to the next guy. But what I noticed was—and it was awesome, horrible—the buildings had collapsed and there was no sign of furniture, desks, people it was all emulsified. Just white dust and white paper. Nothing that you could recognize as part of the building," Hayden recalled.

Working on the mound under generator powered artificial lights was a hazardous business.

"You had to be very careful where you stood, because you did not know how stable the debris pile you were standing on was, and you did not want to fall into the three story deep hole, to the rubble below. Mainly we were looking for bodies, listening to hear if someone was screaming, looking to see if there was movement."

They would eventually be rewarded.

"There were three times when everything stopped— without any signal to stop—and that was when they found either a body or a part of a body. Everyone who was there—there was no conversation—I didn't know who the person to my right was or to my left. It was grim stone-faced work, and somehow—without knowing how—electricity would go through that crowd and everyone would stand up straight and watch and four or five members of the FDNY would pass by us carrying a flag draped stretcher with full honors. And everyone there would stand at attention and put their hand over their heart or salute. Once that treasured item moved out of sight then all work started again." They learned later that one of those stretchers carried a survivor.

Around 5:00 A.M. the team heard that a restaurant that had stayed open, and they drove up to the upscale "Tavern on the Green" in Central Park.

"The place was occupied by hundreds of young people—college people—and when we walked in everyone in the place stood up and cheered. They gave up their tables; they came over and hugged us and kissed us. And the management came over and made sandwiches which we took with us. I was really proud to see our people who sometimes seem not all that patriotic, just behave so magnificently," Hayden recalled.

On the morning of the third day, more volunteers started to come in. The city started to go back to work and so it was time to leave.

The team got turned around on the way home and ended up at Orient Point at the eastern end of Long Island, where they had to take a ferry over to New London.

"We pulled in a line of eight or ten cars, and we went to buy the tickets. They looked at us. We were all nasty looking, and they asked us if we had just come from Ground Zero and we said yes. They said your money's no good here. And everyone clapped and they stopped all the traffic and they pulled us in front of everybody. No one was upset. They were so grateful that we were there," Da Luca said. When the team returned home they quietly went back to work.

"You know the idea that we went up there and made a big difference. Did we? No. But we did what we were supposed to do. We went up there to help and we got involved. I talked to my brothers and sisters about this and we—the whole country was frustrated—the helplessness was crazy—and we felt that we did something, in some way, shape or form it was some kind of an event that helped us to deal with it because we got to go and do it. We didn't do a heck of a lot," said DeLuca.

"The boots that I wore have never been washed because they are still covered with what I call 'sacred dust,'" said Hayden.

The Night They Brought the Kerosene

Bob Criso

"MY LIFE WAS THREATENED," SAID RETURNED Peace Corps Volunteer (RPCV) Bob Criso, his voice cracking as he stood at the podium at the U Mass Boston campus in the shadow of the President John F. Kennedy Library, the striking I.M Pei building on Boston's waterfront. Outside, the sun was bright against the deep blue waters of Boston Harbor lapping at the edges of Columbia Point landscaped with pine trees, shrubs and wild roses reminiscent of the landscape of Cape Cod familiar to President Kennedy.

Color slides flashed on the screen to the side and behind the podium where Criso stood at the head of the large dimly lit conference room. Pictures flashed of a village cut out of the dense equatorial rain forest of West Africa where Criso served. Among those seated at our table were John Bewick, an RPCV from Hingham and his wife, Martha, and Fr. Liam Scanlan, a former missionary in Nigeria, who was spending the summer assisting at St. Anthony's in Cohasset.

A TIME FOR WAR

Criso's presentation was one of a series on an agenda that ranged from current micro-lending projects in Nigeria to readings by Nigerian poet Ifeanyi Menkiti from his published works. It was a reunion of 110 former Peace Corps volunteers who served in Nigeria, West Africa, from not long after the country became independent from Great Britain on October 1, 1960, until 1968 when the country devolved into a civil war that many would come to term an attempted genocide of the Igbo people of Southeastern Nigeria.

Criso was flashing back to July 1967 and his service teaching English in Ishiagu, located in the then Eastern Region of Nigeria, where the predominant ethnic group was Christian, primarily Roman Catholic.

"I was writing essay questions on the blackboard when we heard the hum of the motors outside. Suddenly, two jeeps filled with soldiers in khaki uniforms screeched to a halt outside the classroom door. The bayonets on the soldiers' rifles pointed up like an iron fence. A portly officer with a red braid resting on the shiny black brim of his cap stepped out and met me at the door…'This school will be closed immediately. All students must return to their villages.'" War had come to Ishiagu. Like other Peace Corps volunteers, Criso had not paid much attention to the rumors "that white mercenaries and spies were posing as Peace Corps volunteers."

Criso was suppressing deep emotions as he stood at the podium speaking of those chaotic days so long ago. He recounted his friendship with "the five Igbo teachers: Ekuma, Ugwu, Otu, Chiukwu and Onuhs," who were his fellow teachers at the same school. "We spent many evenings in each other's tiny living rooms, sitting around a dim kerosene lamp, drinking sweet but potent palm wine and swapping stories about our lives and countries." Criso looked to the screen set behind him on the stage where the picture of a large hut flashed. "I lived in a red wooden house built on stilts, previously used by a foreman at a nearby copper mine. During the rainy season, tropical storms pounded the corrugated tin roof like roaring drums. The water emptied into a cement tank that supplied me through the dry season. Fresh papaya and pineapple were abundant. Goat meat and chicken were a luxury. Ejiims, my smiley houseboy, prepared meals on two burners fueled by a gas tank."

But rumors of pogroms in the Muslim north against Ibos living there were spreading south. "The villagers in Ishiagu panicked when refugees returned home from the north with horrific stories of Igbos being 'chopped up.'"

Fear shattered the peaceful existence. Travel in the Peace Corps van became increasingly dangerous as armed men challenged all travelers, especially foreigners. Criso recalled one memorable return from a harrowing but necessary errand: "Minutes after arriving back at my house, strangers began to gather outside. Within an hour, the house was surrounded by what looked like an angry mob of twenty-something men and women. Some were holding machetes, crude clubs or broken tree branches. Two muscular young men in threadbare shorts and T-shirts came to the front door. Ejiims and I met them there…A few minutes later, two men rolled a rusty, blue, fifty-gallon kerosene drum under the center of the house…It started

Bob Criso visting China, 2015

to rain. Outside I saw Obi, an elder from the village, climbing onto a tree stump to the side of the mob. Dressed in traditional tribal robes with a bold, brown and white tropical print design, he addressed the crowd calmly but firmly. 'This man has been our friend and contributed much to this community. Come to your senses....' The crowd began to thin out. The kerosene drum remained."

Criso recalled the sleepless night ending with screeching brakes in front of his house. "Soldiers again! But I felt immediate relief when I realized the thin white woman with the straw hat sitting in the back seat of one of two jeeps was Barbara, the Peace Corps nurse."

"'Let's go, Bob. No packing. The others are gone. There's a boat in Port Harcourt waiting for us.' We left immediately." To this day Criso regrets there was no time for farewells to fellow teachers and his students. Unrest was rising, as were roadblocks. The window of escape was closing.

When Criso returned in November 2008 to Ishiagu with a group of RPVCs, he was delighted to be reunited with a former student, Fabian Nwachukwu. "Fabian filled me in on some of the missing years. He was an officer during the war, forced to kill on the front lines. 'It was kill or be killed,' Fabian recalled of his war service." Criso learned the sad fate of his former colleagues and students: Patrick, fought as a soldier; Leonard hid in the bush for three years until the war was over; and Celestine, the school's most gifted student, had been killed during the war. Two of his teacher colleagues had been killed and two had gone missing.

Recoiling from the news, Criso accompanied by Fabian returned to the old classroom where so many years before the jeeps had pulled up. "The blackboard where I had written the essay questions was cracked and worn. We pulled a desk into the dusty room and Fabian sat in his familiar seat, the far right end of the first row. I stood in front of the blackboard and he raised his hand as if asking a question." The screen flashed a picture of a smiling middle-aged African facing the audience with raised hand. "We had someone take a picture."

A TIME FOR WAR

Warrior among Diplomats: Scituate's Four Star US Army Chief of Staff

General George Casey, Jr., USA (RET)

"I WAS THINKING OF A CAREER IN THE State Department when I entered The Edmund G. Walsh Foreign Service School at Georgetown University in 1966," said recently retired Army Chief of Staff George Casey, Jr. "The plan was after graduation with a degree in International Relations to complete my obligation under Army ROTC, and then get out of the Army to go to law school."

Casey, who has a home in Scituate near his mother, was born in Sendai, Japan. His father, George Casey, Sr., a West Point graduate, was at that time a young Army officer serving in Japan as part of the occupation force immediately following the end of World War II.

"I attended four high schools in three different countries and graduated from Boston College High in 1966. So the combination of enjoying foreign countries

General George Casey, Jr. in 2007.

and the love of history, were motivations for me to go to Georgetown."

"I was commissioned a 2nd lieutenant on the 6th of June, 1970." By then, George Casey, Sr. was a two star general and commander of the First Air Cavalry Division in Vietnam.

"One morning about a month later my mother called me to tell me he was missing. Finally, two days later when I went in to work, there was the *Washington Post* on a table and his picture was on the front page. My father was killed on the 7th of July, 1970. He had just taken over the 1st cavalry division which was operating in the Parrot Beak area (near the Cambodian border). As part of the wrap-up he was on his way from field headquarters to Cam Ranh Bay to visit wounded soldiers when his helicopter flew into a cloud in a valley and as they attempted to climb out they hit the top of the mountain."

In October of 1970, Casey was assigned to Ft. Benning, Georgia, for officer basic training, jump school, and then to a mortar platoon as part of the 2nd Battalion (509TH) Airborne and Mechanized Infantry in Germany. The plan was to serve in Germany for a year and then go to Vietnam. But the Pentagon started scaling down in Vietnam, and Casey's tour in Europe was extended to forty-two months.

"When you come in as a lieutenant all you want to be is company commander, so I did that. My first command as a company commander was in Ft. Carson, Colorado. I really loved it."

Casey's plans of a career in the Foreign Service soon changed. "In my first assignment I realized the men are dependent on you for their survival. And once I had that realization I vowed to never let my subordinates down. That became the thing that drove me throughout my career."

There was a point early in his Army service when Casey was in Fort Carson, Colorado and realized he wanted to make a change. "I was in an infantry battalion for the first eight years. And after a while you kind of get fed up. I was getting tired of colonels who did not seem to be interested in anything that I considered important, like training, but were more interested in administrative details. At that point I started to ask myself is this all the Army was about. I was seriously thinking about doing something else when I got a call from my detailer who asked me, 'We have this fully funded program, and would you like to go to graduate school on the Army?'"

It was at this point where his interest in international matters and diplomacy merged with his choice of the Army as his career. He entered the Korvell School of International Studies at the nearby University of Denver.

"I was going to be a Northeast Asian foreign area officer. The university offered a course in Northeast Asian (Japan, China, Korea) studies so it was a perfect fit." Accepting the offer of an eighteen months graduate program entailed an additional three year obligation to the Army.

"So I went up there and had a wonderful experience. It was one of the two most broadening experiences that I had as young officer. And after that the Army kept giving me interesting challenges."

After completing the graduate school program, Casey was supposed to go to the Foreign Service language school to study Japanese for two years. "I got a call from my detailer saying, 'We have an opening at the UN truce supervision organization in Jerusalem. Are you interested?'"

From 1980 to 1981 Casey served on the United Nations Truce Supervision Organization (UNTSO) located in Egypt, Lebanon, Israel and Syria. "I spent a year in Cairo working with a multinational peace keeping force in which there were 200 observers under the command of an Irish lieutenant colonel. We would go out to man the observation posts in the Sinai to try to keep Egypt and Israel from going to war again. By then I had been promoted to major. I was at the parade with my family when President Sadat was shot."

It was at Sadat's funeral where he met Egypt's Hosni Mubarak.

After completing his tour with UNTSO, Casey returned to Ft. Carson for field grade branch qualification where he became executive officer of the battalion. His next assignment was as secretary to the general staff of the 4th Infantry Division.

"I was there for three years and I was getting ready to leave and I came out on the command list. I was promoted to lieutenant colonel and in 1985 took over the 1st Battalion, 10th infantry, mechanized," where he served for two years.

The theme of the Army giving Casey interesting assignments continued. "The normal progression is to go from command to a war college. I was selected to attend a fellowship at the Atlantic Council of the United States, a NATO support organization. There were about thirty fellowships in the entire Army. And that was the second most broadening experience that I had, and it was in Washington, DC."

In the program, wearing civilian clothes, Casey said, "We had access to go anywhere in the government we wanted to go, to concentrate on an area. I was exposed to the think tanks in DC. I got connected with one of the members who was working on a paper on the conventional balance of forces between the U.S .and the Warsaw Pac.

This was in 1987 when we were just starting to recognize that the Warsaw Pac may not quite be the imposing force we thought it was—that indeed we may have some advantages."

Having completed that assignment, Casey was told by his detailer to find a job at the Pentagon. "I found a job at the Pentagon working as an Army legislative assistant with Congress. I reported to a two-star general who was the head of the legislative liaison program. I started out in operations, budget, the INF (Intermediate-Range Nuclear Forces) Treaty, and strategy, so I had a very diverse portfolio." He was asked to serve on the staff of the chief of staff of the Army, where his responsibilities included congressional and international security policy.

"Then I was selected to be the chief of staff of the 1st Cavalry Division in Ft. Hood, Texas. In 1991 I came out as brigade commander."

Service in the Balkans followed in March of 1995. In July of 1999, Casey became commander of the 1st Armored Division and served in that capacity until he was appointed to serve in the Pentagon as the Director of Strategic Plans and Policy until January 2003 when he was made director of the Joint Staff.

Casey was promoted to senior commander of coalition forces in Iraq and served there for two and half years (June 2004 to February 2007) where his life-long interest in diplomacy served him well in working with the various leaders of the government there. In that capacity he led the effort to train Iraqi forces so that they might be able to take on the work that was being done by the American Army. He also worked closely with American diplomats on the issue of holding free elections.

Casey's concern for his troops extends to championing a program designed to prepare them physically and mentally for re-integration into civilian life after they return home.

He ended his military career serving as Chief of Staff of the Army retiring in June 2011.

"They have a wonderful Fathers' Day ceremony at the Vietnam Memorial Wall where people from all over the country can go online and coordinate for a rose to be placed at their fathers name. I belong to that organization. My father's name is on nine west on the Wall."

Casey is a summer resident of Scituate; he lives with his wife Sheila and they have two sons, Sean and Ryan.

A TIME FOR WAR

About the Author

R ONALD WHEATLEY WAS BORN IN LOS ANGELES, California. He is a practicing attorney living in Scituate (by the sea), Massachusetts.

After graduating from Gonzaga University in Spokane, Washington, Mr. Wheatley joined the Peace Corps and served as a Peace Corps volunteer in Nigeria, West Africa for two years in the mid 1960s. His first book, *A Song of Africa*, is based on his experience in Nigeria when the country became embroiled in a bloody civil war. He has traveled widely throughout West Africa.

Following his return to the United States, he taught for one year at an inner city junior high school in Tacoma, Washington. In 1966 he made an existential decision and volunteered for the draft. In September 1966 he was drafted and did his basic training at Ft. Lewis, Washington, and then to signals school at Ft. Huachuca, Arizona. Mr. Wheatley served in Vietnam with the 1st Signal Brigade from 1967-68.

Ronald Wheatley is also the author of *The Trial of Phillis Wheatley*, a docudrama produced at Bridgewater State University in Bridgewater, MA. It was published in January 2014 and is now available on Amazon in book and Kindle formats.

Mr. Wheatley is a member of the Massachusetts Society of the Sons of the American Revolution.